"Life is like a wheel. Sooner or later, it always comes around to where you started again."

—STEPHEN KING

Whistle Stop Café Mysteries

SOONER
or LATER

BETH ADAMS

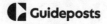

Cover and interior design by Müllerhaus
Cover illustration by Greg Copeland at Illustration Online LLC.
Typeset by Aptara, Inc.

ISBN 978-1-961441-14-9 (hardcover)
ISBN 978-1-961441-15-6 (epub)

Printed and bound in the United States of America
10 9 8 7 6 5 4 3 2 1

SOONER or LATER

CHAPTER ONE

*J*anet Shaw was just about finished wiping down the counters when Debbie Albright's phone rang. It was a gray March Monday, with bitter wind whipping around outside, but it was cozy and warm inside the Whistle Stop Café. The lunch rush was over, and they were almost finished cleaning up. They had just sent Paulette Connor, who waited tables for them, home, and Janet looked forward to her afternoon plans. As the bleat of Debbie's cell phone sounded again, Debbie rested her broom against the wall of the dining room and pulled the phone out of her pocket.

"Hey there," Debbie said into the phone.

It was Greg. Janet could tell just by the way Debbie's voice softened and her lips curled up into a smile. Debbie and Greg Connor had been dating for several months, and just a few weeks ago Greg had proposed. Janet couldn't be happier for her best friend, and she loved seeing how Debbie lit up whenever Greg called.

"What?" Debbie said into the phone. "That's crazy."

Janet couldn't hear what Greg was saying, but whatever it was, Debbie was obviously surprised.

"Where?"

Janet finished wiping the counter and rinsed out her rag in the bucket of warm water, watching Debbie the whole time. Janet had already stacked the leftover pastries and wrapped them to take home, and Debbie had broken down the register and transferred the cash to the safe in the office. Janet had also taken copies of many of the recipes they used in the kitchen at various points in the day while her partner was busy with other tasks. As soon as Debbie finished in the dining room, they should be ready to head out.

"I can't believe it," Debbie was saying. "I think there is one, but I don't know if it's the right kind or if it works. I can ask Kim and let you know." After another pause she said, "Okay. I'll go talk to her now and then update you."

She ended the call and turned to Janet. "That was Greg."

"I'd gathered that. What's going on?"

"He's renovating the old theater over on Grant."

"I wondered what was happening there. Is someone actually going to turn it back into a theater again?" The old building must have been beautiful once, but the marquee outside the long low brick building had long since been battered and broken, and the building abandoned. Janet remembered the space being used as a discount clothing store and a short-lived bank over the years. For a while a church had met there, until they'd built their own building outside of town. But mostly it had sat empty, an eyesore.

"Jim Watson's brother Sam bought it," Debbie said. Jim was the editor of the *Gazette*, the local newspaper. "He plans to turn it back into a theater, and Greg is working on the renovations."

"That's wonderful. It will be so nice to have a local theater again." Greg was a contractor, and he would do a great job restoring the old place. "But it sounds like something exciting happened in the process?"

"Greg said he was knocking down some walls today, and in the space inside one wall, he found some old film canisters. Like, movie film strips. One of the canisters has a date written on it—September 1944."

"Whoa. I knew that theater was old, but I didn't know it was that old."

"I think Greg said it opened back in the thirties originally. Obviously it underwent a lot of changes as technology progressed, but anyway, it's possible that at least one of the rolls of film could actually be from the forties. He thought he remembered seeing an old film projector at the museum, and wondered if it might still work."

"Huh. There is one there, right?" Janet could picture the hulking machine. It was in one of the back rooms of the museum, in a display about films centered on World War II. "Does it work?"

"I have no idea, but I said I would ask Kim. I haven't seen her yet today, so I don't know if she's around."

The museum was closed on Mondays, but this sounded like the kind of thing Kim Smith would be excited about. "Let's give her a call. If it is old film from the forties, she'll be interested to learn more."

Debbie nodded and pulled up the Dennison Depot Museum director's phone number and made the call. Janet listened in on Debbie's end of the conversation as she explained what Greg had found and what they were looking for. When Debbie hung up, she had a smile on her face.

"She was at home and said this is much more interesting than folding laundry. She'll be right over. I'll tell Greg to bring the film here."

Janet hesitated. What she was about to say seemed kind of crazy, but she decided to just say it. "You don't think there's any chance it's *that* film, do you?"

"The Clark Gable film?" Debbie asked. The fact that Debbie knew what she was talking about meant that she'd thought of it too.

"Didn't it disappear about that time?" Janet had heard about the film star's visit to Dennison many times over the years. Clark Gable, one of Hollywood's biggest celebrities, had been born in nearby Cadiz and enlisted in the army during World War II. After he'd been discharged from active military duty, he'd come back to Ohio and spent nearly two weeks in Dennison, filming footage for a movie he planned to make about the war effort on the home front. But after a week and a half of shooting, the film was stolen from his hotel room and never recovered. The project was abandoned, the star left town, and the missing film had never been found. Many of the older residents in town still referenced the star's visit to Dennison from time to time, and they'd all heard the story.

"I think 1944 was about the time the film was stolen, if I'm remembering correctly," Debbie said. "I don't know. I guess what Greg found could be that film, but it doesn't make any sense. How would it have ended up inside the wall of the theater in Dennison if it was the film stolen from Clark Gable?"

"I don't know," Janet said. "I guess we'll have to see what it is if we can get the projector working."

By the time Janet and Debbie had finished cleaning up the café, Kim had arrived, and Janet and Debbie walked through the old station waiting room and into the entrance to the museum. Kim greeted them, flipped on the overhead lights, and then led them through the quiet museum to one of the rooms at the back.

"Here it is," Kim said, gesturing at a large machine that was nearly the size of a person. The top part was a metal case with a series of lenses at the front. The bottom was a large metal box, where Janet assumed the motor was housed.

"I knew I'd seen it here," Debbie said.

"Does it work?" Janet asked.

"It's supposed to," Kim said. "It's a 1940s-era 35 mm projector. I rescued it from the old theater decades ago, back when they were turning it into a bank. It had been sitting in the basement in storage for years, and Stanley said it should still work, but to be honest I've never tried it."

"Stanley?" Debbie blinked.

"Stanley Hersey," Kim said. "He owned the theater until it closed in the eighties."

Janet had heard that name before. She thought Stanley was the father of Max Hersey, her dad's childhood friend.

"He was clearing out the storage rooms before he sold the building," Kim continued. "I swooped in to rescue as much as I could. This beauty was a real modern marvel in her day. Let's see if we can fire her up."

Kim unlocked the glass case that held the projector. Janet looked at the display around it and saw that it showcased stories of Hollywood stars who were also active-duty service members. There was a black-and-white photo of Jimmy Stewart in his army uniform, and the paragraphs underneath the photo discussed the film star's illustrious military career. Stewart, Janet read, was already a big star when he'd enlisted in the army in 1941, and he'd fought in the European theater during the war. He'd retired from the military as a Brigadier General, making him the highest-ranking actor in American military history. There were also sections of the display dedicated to Audie Murphy, Bea Arthur, and, well, Clark Gable. Gable, the display said, had joined the army in 1942, after his wife Carole Lombard died, and served until June of 1944. His visit to Dennison had been shortly after that.

Kim reached for the big machine, positioning her hands on it one way, then another, and then paused.

"How heavy is this thing?" Debbie asked.

"Very," Kim said. "I'm not sure the best way to pull it out of here."

"I can help with that." They all turned around at the sound of the deep voice, and Janet saw Greg Connor and Sam Watson striding toward them down the hallway. Sam had two thin, round containers of film about the size of an apple pie under his arm. "The door was unlocked. I hope it's okay that we let ourselves in," Greg said.

"Of course," Kim said. "I'm glad you're here."

They stopped just in front of the display case and surveyed the machine. Greg was tall, with broad shoulders and dark hair lightly threaded with gray. Sam Watson was shorter and stockier, with curly hair fading to gray, though it must once have been blond.

"How about if I grab the bottom and you take the top?" Greg said.

"Let's try it." Sam held out the film canisters, and Janet took them from him. The blue-green metal of the cases was cool under her skin. Janet saw that the top canister had *#1, September 1944* written on it in black ink, and the second had simply *#2*. There was nothing else on the outside to indicate what was on the film or where it had come from. Then Sam stepped toward the projector, Greg counted to three, and together they hoisted the machine out of the display case and set it on the floor.

"Where would you like it?" Greg asked.

"Let's not try to move it far," Kim said. She pointed to a section of the opposite wall where there was an open white space. "Can you turn it that way, and we can try to see if it will project there?"

"Sure thing." The men lifted the machine once more and positioned it so the lenses faced the open space. Kim ran to the storage room to get an extension cord—"Make sure it has a surge protector!" Greg insisted—and after she plugged it in, they were all more than surprised when a square of white light appeared on the far wall.

"It actually turned on," Debbie said.

"Now let's see if we can figure out how to get the film into it," Kim said. She pressed a button on the side of the machine, and the top part opened. Inside there was a piece that pulled out that had two wheels. It looked kind of like the old film projectors Janet remembered viewing educational films on in the classroom when she was a child.

"That's got to be where the film goes," she said, and Debbie nodded.

"But how do we get it in there?" Kim said.

It took about fifteen minutes of trial and error, but eventually they had one of the rolls of film, the one labeled 1944, loaded into the wheels, and they carefully closed the machine.

"Here goes nothing," Kim said, and pressed another button on the side of the machine to start it. When a black-and-white image of a young Eileen Palmer appeared on the screen, they all cheered, and Kim let out a whoop. Eileen wore the dark jacket and hat from her time as the stationmaster at the Dennison Depot. Sam ran over to the light switch and flipped off the overhead lights.

"It's Mom!" Kim said, clapping.

On the screen, Eileen waved, standing in what looked like the door of a train car. The film was grainy by today's standards, but you could make out what was on the screen easily enough.

"Can you tell us how long you've been the stationmaster here at the Dennison Depot?" asked a voice off camera. Janet looked over at Debbie, whose eyes widened. That voice was familiar.

"I took over about a year ago, when the regular stationmaster was called into active military duty," Eileen said. "I was a volunteer here at the canteen before that."

Janet had seen photos of Eileen during her time as stationmaster before, but she'd never seen video footage. It was amazing to see and hear her like this.

"What does a stationmaster do?" the off-screen voice said. Janet felt a shiver of recognition. She knew that voice. At one point, most people in America would have recognized that voice.

On-screen, Eileen talked about how she was responsible for making sure the trains arrived and left as scheduled, how she oversaw safety in the station, and how she looked after the workers, including the porters and the ticket sellers.

"How old are you, Miss Turner?"

"Almost twenty-one."

"It's pretty amazing that someone as young as you are manages this whole station."

"There's a war on. We all have to step up and do our part, and if this is how I can best serve my country, I'm proud to do it," Eileen said. It was incredible to see her so young and full of life, but that wasn't what captivated Janet most about the interview. Was she crazy? Was her mind playing tricks on her because she wanted to believe it was Clark Gable interviewing Eileen?

Janet wasn't a huge film buff, but she'd gone through a classic movie phase in high school and had fallen in love with famous actors of the times. Cary Grant, Sidney Poitier, Clark Gable. For Janet, Clark Gable was especially easy on the eyes. Could it really be Hollywood's biggest star behind the camera on this film?

The interview with Eileen lasted about ten minutes, and then it cut off. Then the camera was instead pointed into the canteen—now the Whistle Stop Café—where volunteers were packing lunches into paper bags by the hundreds. Janet and Debbie both clapped to see their familiar café as it had been back in the forties, when it was the home of the volunteer effort to feed the service personnel who came through Dennison on their way to war.

"Look how great the windows are!" Debbie said.

"And the ceilings! That pressed tin looks so good," Janet added.

"I love the women's outfits," Kim added.

Janet had to admit the outfits in the forties were pretty much the best. The women all wore demure dresses, some with full skirts, as well as dressy shoes and swirled updos. Janet couldn't imagine getting dressed up that nicely for much of anything, let alone a day of making sandwiches.

The man behind the camera started talking to one of the women packing lunches. The woman was tall with dark hair, and she wore a no-nonsense button-down dress. She looked familiar, though Janet couldn't place her. There was a young girl, maybe a preteen, by her side, with curly dark hair and a wide smile. It took a minute for Janet to realize she knew who the young girl was.

"Is that Gayle?" She turned to Debbie. "Ray Zink's sister?"

Debbie looked closer then said, "Oh my. Yes, I think it is."

Gayle Zink—now Gayle Bailey—lived in Columbus and was still spry and energetic, even in her nineties. It was surprising to see her here, so young and vibrant. The woman next to her had to be her mother, judging by the similarity in their faces and countenance. On-screen, the mother talked about how every day the women of Dennison came to the depot and volunteered their time to feeding and welcoming the soldiers who passed through. Seeing Gayle come alive on film was incredible. It was so fun seeing a younger version of their friend that for a moment, she forgot why they were viewing the footage at all, until the familiar voice asked the women to show him the doughnut fryer, and Janet wondered, once again, whether it truly could be Clark Gable. The voice was so familiar—but did she just *want* it to be him?

The scene in the canteen lasted a few minutes longer, and when the film cut off, the scene shifted, and they saw the inside of an ornate building. It had sumptuous wallpaper and paintings edged with scrolled gilt frames and heavy red drapery. A sparkling chandelier hung from the middle of the room. At first Janet thought it must be a ballroom, but then she saw a counter, backed by mirrors and a case of popcorn, at the far end.

"A theater?" Debbie guessed.

"Wait, is that—"

"That's it!" Sam exclaimed. "That's my theater!"

"Oh my," Janet said. "I don't remember it looking like that, that's for sure." The theater had closed its doors when Janet and Debbie were very young. Janet had a vague memory of having been here once, to see the movie *Annie* with her mother, so that must have been in the early eighties or so. She remembered plush carpets and seats and the smell of popcorn, and the sense that the building was enormous, but that was pretty much all she could call to mind.

"I think a lot of the grandeur had faded by the time you went there," Sam said.

"Look at that concession stand." Debbie shook her head. "That looks like wood."

"That's still there, such as it is," Sam said.

A man walked into the shot and addressed the camera. "My name is Stanley Hersey, and I'm the owner of Sunshine Cinemas."

"Mr. Hersey, can you tell us what it's been like to own a theater since the war started?" the familiar voice asked.

"Well, it's been tough, of course," Stanley said. "On the one hand, Americans need distraction, and there are plenty of good films being produced. On the other hand, so many men are overseas fighting that it's hard to sell enough tickets sometimes. Of course, all soldiers returning from war get a free movie ticket here at Sunshine Cinemas, yourself included." He ducked his head at the camera.

"Why, thank you very much. I will take you up on that offer."

"It would be an honor, Mr. Gable."

A man stepped into the shot from off-screen and reached out and shook the theater owner's hand, and everyone in the room gasped.

There he was. He was instantly recognizable, standing in front of the camera. There was no mistaking that smile, that signature mustache. Standing in the lobby of the old theater was Hollywood legend Clark Gable.

Which meant that this was very likely part of the film project he had shot in Dennison in 1944. The film reels that had been reported stolen.

So how had they ended up buried in the wall of the old theater?

CHAPTER TWO

Wait. Is this—" Kim began, at the same time Debbie said, "It's one of the stolen film reels!"

Kim searched the outside of the machine, and Janet guessed she was looking for a way to pause the film. There didn't seem to be one, and so they all watched as Gable spoke into the camera, talking about how the special town of Dennison had rallied behind the war effort. After he finished speaking, the shot cut off, and the screen went black. A moment later, the end of the reel of film began flapping against the side of the machine. Kim reached over and switched it off. Sam flipped the overhead lights back on.

"I had heard about this," Greg said. "About Clark Gable and the film that was stolen from him here. But I had no idea it was actually real."

Janet felt the same way. Growing up in Dennison, she'd heard stories about Clark Gable's visit to the town as well, about the movie he'd been making, and about the unsolved mystery of the movie that never was. Still, she had never quite grasped that the biggest star in Hollywood truly had been here in Dennison for a time, talking to the people she knew and loved. It must have been exciting. Thrilling. And it must have been devastating when the film was stolen.

"How in the world did it end up in the theater?" Sam asked. "Has it been there this whole time?"

"I guess it must have," Greg said. "Where we found it, it wasn't like that area was accessible to anyone. It had been sealed up for decades, at least. If we hadn't knocked down that wall, I wonder if anyone would have ever found it."

"But if it really is Clark Gable's stolen film, we need to report it to the police," Kim said.

"Good thinking," Debbie said. "Maybe it can be returned to—well, I guess not to him."

Janet nodded. She didn't know when Gable had died, but she was pretty sure it was many decades past.

"But someone will want it," Kim said. "If it really is his."

"I'll call Ian." Janet's husband Ian was the Chief of Police for the town of Dennison. He would know what to do with it.

Janet stepped into the next room. Ian picked up on the third ring.

"Hey. What's up?" he asked.

"I'm at the museum, and we have something…strange."

"Why am I not surprised?"

Janet told him about the film and where the footage had been found, and then he asked her to repeat it all.

"You're saying you found old film reels that you think were stolen from Clark Gable in 1944 behind one of the walls of the old theater?"

"Well, *I* didn't find them, but yes, that's the gist of it."

"If you're right and that's truly what this is, the statute of limitations for theft has long passed."

Janet knew that Ian was in the middle of a big case. They were working to bring down a local drug distributor, and getting very close to being able to make an arrest. On top of that, Captain Hernandez, one of the force's most trusted and valued officers, was on paternity leave, so Ian was short staffed.

"Yes, but if we're right and that's truly what this is, there will be a lot of people who will be very interested in seeing this."

Ian let out a long breath. "All right. I'll come down and check it out."

"Thanks, hon." She ended the call and went back to the room where the others were trying to load the second reel of film into the machine. "Ian is on his way."

"In that case, let's see what's on this film before he takes it away," Kim said, and closed up the machine again. The lights went off, and the film started rolling.

The scene that appeared on the screen was an image of a train steaming into the Dennison station. People on the platform scurried around as it rolled to a stop. Moments later, the doors of the train were thrown open and soldiers in uniform began to step out onto the platform, stretching their arms and striding toward the station. They looked so young. Most of them were no older than Janet's daughter Tiffany was now, and heading off to face who knew what. How many of those brave young men had made it home? At least no matter what else they were going to face, they were welcomed and treated to good food and friendly smiles here in Dennison.

"Probably footage he was planning to use to string scenes together," Sam said, and Greg agreed.

After a few minutes of that footage, the scene cut to inside the café again, and this time, the footage showed soldiers being handed lunch bags. After a few minutes of this, the scene once again cut away, now moving to outside the station, where more volunteers were frying doughnuts in hot oil. Janet and Debbie still used the same recipe when they made doughnuts for special occasions at the café.

Interviews with several soldiers followed, including one with a young army private named Danny Maldanado, who identified himself as being from Dennison. He had dark hair and big eyes and didn't look a day past eighteen.

"How are you feeling as you head off to join your unit?" Gable asked from off-screen.

"I'm proud to serve my country," Danny said.

"Are you nervous at all?"

Danny hesitated a moment, and the fear that passed over his face was palpable. But he said, "No, sir. So many good people have joined up and risked their lives in this fight, and I am proud to be one of them."

"I don't know that I could be that brave," Debbie said when the scene cut off.

"Unless I'm mistaken, Danny Maldanado is one of the names on the war memorial here in town," Kim said.

"Oh." Janet knew what that meant instantly. "So he didn't make it."

"He was killed in battle," Kim confirmed.

Janet pressed her lips together to fight the tears that rose up. The image of the young man on that screen, headed off to a war from which he wouldn't return home, was almost too much.

"I wonder if the family still lives in town," Kim said. "They might like to see—"

But the scene shifted, and there were several more moving interviews with soldiers passing through town. There were also interviews with the minister of the Methodist church in town and members of the ladies' auxiliary and several more volunteers at the depot.

Then the scene changed again, and this time the film showed the inside of a large, high-ceilinged room with a long wooden desk. The rows of cubbies behind the desk, the pegboard of metal keys, and the man in a suit with a porter's hat marked this as a hotel. Couples glided in and out over a thick Oriental rug.

"Is that in Dennison?" Janet asked. She'd never seen anything as upscale as this.

"I have no idea," Debbie said. "It doesn't look like anything I've ever seen here."

The camera moved closer to the front desk, and the man looked up and smiled. "Good afternoon, Mr. Gable," he said. The man had a waxed mustache, glasses, and light-colored hair. He blinked a few times, clearly starstruck. "How can I help you this afternoon?"

"Could you please introduce yourself for the camera?" Clark said.

"My name is Bernard Williams, and I am the manager of the Del Mar hotel here in Dennison," he said.

The Del Mar? Janet had never heard of a hotel by that name in town. It must have closed decades ago.

"I was hoping you could tell me about how the Del Mar is helping with the war effort," Clark said from off-screen.

"Of course, Mr. Gable. The Del Mar is honored to be able to provide rooms, free of charge, to hundreds of soldiers throughout the war. Sometimes train delays lead to soldiers being stranded here overnight, and we've always been happy to provide clean beds and warm meals for the men defending our country. We've also given housing, free of charge, to the families of soldiers returning home for medical care. After the families meet their sons at the Dennison station, we're able to offer them a place to stay until they can start for home."

"That's very impressive."

"We're all doing our part, however we can," Bernard said. "The Del Mar is a world-class establishment, and we're honored to help the war effort."

"It is a very nice hotel," Clark said. "I have to admit, I was surprised to find such a classy establishment here in rural Ohio."

"Dennison is a destination in and of itself, and we're proud to be the leading hotel in the area."

"I didn't know there was once a hotel that nice here in Dennison," Debbie said as the screen faded to black. "I wonder where that was."

"I think it was over on Grant Street," Greg said. "I've seen pictures of it in the Department of Building files. It closed sometime in the fifties or sixties, after a fire, if I'm remembering that right."

"Why was it called the Del Mar?" Debbie asked. "We're in the middle of Ohio. That's a thousand miles from the closest sea."

"No idea," Greg said. "Maybe whoever built it thought it was a funny joke."

"Or maybe they just didn't speak Spanish," Sam said, shrugging.

Janet had thought the film was done, but they all went quiet when another scene began on the screen.

Clark Gable appeared again, this time sitting next to a woman in the vinyl booth of what looked like an old-fashioned diner. A melamine table gleamed in the light from a brass lamp that hung over the table.

"That's the old Delancey Diner," Sam said. "I used to go to that place when I was a kid."

"Who's that woman?" Debbie asked. She looked young, still a teenager, and her eyes were wide, a grin splashed across her face. She wore the fitted dress that said she worked as a waitress at the diner. She was beautiful, whoever she was, with a pert nose and her hair twisted up in shiny rolls.

"What do you like about working at the diner?" Clark said to her. This was different. Most of the interviews they'd seen had had Clark off-screen, but here he was on camera with her. Janet wondered if he'd set the camera on a tripod or hired a cameraman.

The woman thought for half a second and then said, "You meet the most interesting people. You just never know who is going to walk in that door."

Clark laughed. "I suppose that's true."

"But I'm not going to be a waitress forever," she continued. "I'm going to Hollywood. I'm going to be a star just like you."

"Is that right?"

"Don't tell my parents, but I've got plans. I'll be in California by Christmas, one way or another."

"One way or another? That almost sounds like a threat."

"Maybe it is." She laughed. "Like I said, I've been making plans. And I've been putting aside money."

"The tips here must be pretty good if you've been able to save up for a train ticket."

"I didn't say it all came from working here. There are other ways, you know. Though, I will say the tips have gotten bigger since I've been waiting on you."

The woman preened under his attention. "Maybe you and I will star in a movie together someday," she said.

"With that kind of cheek, I suspect you'll go far in Hollywood."

He leaned forward, toward the camera, reaching out his arm. As the scene ended, the film began flopping around the wheel of the projector again.

"I guess he turned the camera off," Janet said.

"He must have. The question is, how did this film, which was supposed to have been stolen from Clark Gable's room, probably inside that very hotel, end up in the wall of the movie theater?" Debbie asked.

"The police must have done a full investigation, back in the day," Janet said.

"I'm sure they did," Debbie said. "They no doubt turned over every stone for someone like Clark Gable. But obviously they never recovered the film."

Janet glanced at Debbie and wondered if her friend was thinking the same thing she was.

"I'm curious if records of the original investigation still exist somewhere," Janet said.

Just then, Janet's phone buzzed. She looked down and saw that she had a text from Ian. I'M OUTSIDE THE MUSEUM.

"He's here. I'll go meet him and bring him in," Janet said.

Janet walked back through the rooms of the museum and out the front door. The bitter wind whipped through her hair. Ian stood outside, his wool coat pulled tight around him. "Come on in," she said.

Ian followed her inside. "How do you always manage to find the most interesting things?" he asked as he stepped in after her, letting the door close behind him.

"I had nothing to do with this one," Janet said. "Greg found it. Debbie and I just helped locate the machine that could play the film."

"Did you get it to work?"

"We did. Wait till you see it." Janet led him through the museum to the back room, where someone had flipped the overhead lights on. Greg and Sam told Ian where they'd found the film canisters and what they suspected they might be.

"I can't believe you got this old thing to work," Ian said, walking over to examine the machine.

"I can't believe it either," Kim said. "But we did, and watching it, it's pretty clear that what Greg and Sam suggested was right. Clark Gable appears in this footage, and even when he's not on camera, it's his voice you can hear."

"Really?" Ian cocked his head.

"I'd always assumed the story was one of those urban legends, to be honest," Sam said. "I mean, sure, I'd heard rumors that Clark Gable had come to town and made a movie, and that the footage disappeared, but I've also been to enough places where George Washington supposedly slept that I guess I thought it was just a story."

"Oh, no," Kim said. "This story was national news in its day. It definitely wasn't an urban legend."

"Well, after seeing the film, and given where Greg found it, it's pretty hard to discount it now."

"Would you like to see it?" Kim asked Ian, and when he nodded, she reloaded the film and played the first reel, then the other. Janet used the video camera on her phone to record both reels as they played this time. There were over a dozen interviews, some with people who were only just passing through town, but taken altogether, it was a beautiful, emotional collection of clips.

"Wow," Ian said, shaking his head. "And you found this where?"

After Greg and Sam explained again about knocking down the wall, Kim spooled the film back up and loaded the reels back into the metal canisters.

"Just think how big this could be," Debbie said. "This is the footage that was stolen from Clark Gable. Everyone in Hollywood is going to want to see this. Maybe someone could make it into a short film after all. Or a documentary."

Kim held out the canisters to Ian, but he didn't take them.

"I'm not quite sure what to do with this, to be totally honest," Ian said. "Like I told Janet, the statute of limitations on this theft expired decades ago, and the victim has been dead nearly as long."

"Maybe you'll be able to figure out who took it, though," Janet said.

"And get it back to whoever it belongs to," Debbie said.

"I don't know. I'm not sure this is something for the police to take on, to be honest. It's an eighty-year-old case, and while finding these canisters is great, unless there's new evidence to suggest who stole them and put them in the theater, I'm just not sure what we can do with this."

Janet looked at Debbie. She could already tell Debbie was thinking the same thing she was. If Ian didn't want to try to find out what had happened and how the stolen film had ended up in the theater, they would just have to do it themselves.

CHAPTER THREE

Once Sam and Greg had helped return the heavy projector to the display case, Sam held the film canisters, looking down at them.

"I kind of think these should be locked up somewhere," he said.

"I should say so," Greg said. "Given what we know they are, you should keep them safe."

"But I don't have a safe place to keep them, unfortunately."

"We have a safe at the café, if you want to put them there for now," Debbie volunteered. "Just until you figure out what you want to do with them."

"Seriously? That would be great." They all walked out of the museum. Kim locked it up, and Debbie went into the café to store both film canisters in the safe. When she came back out, Greg looked over at Sam. "Okay if I come back to the theater to finish up?"

Sam laughed. "I don't think I've ever had a contractor ask to stay and work at a project longer," he said. "Of course. That would be great. The sooner the work gets done, the sooner we can open."

"Could we come too?" Debbie asked.

As soon as she heard her friend voice the question, Janet realized she wanted to go too. Right now all she knew was that the film had been behind a wall in the old theater, but she couldn't really visualize it. It would help to be able to see it.

"You want to see the theater?" Greg asked.

Debbie nodded. "I would love to see where the film was found, if that's okay."

"Why not?" Sam said. "As long as you're okay with it."

"It's a construction site," Greg said. "So it doesn't look like much at the moment."

"That's all right," Janet said quickly.

"Let's go." Greg looked over at Debbie. "Do you want to ride with me?"

"Sure."

Debbie hopped in Greg's truck, and Janet followed behind them in her own car as they drove the short distance to the old theater. It sat on a commercial street at the edge of the downtown area, surrounded by a mix of empty storefronts and thrift stores, take-out places, and an old scuzzy bar. It was a wide building, with an art deco-style marquee that had long since been painted over. Some of the panels were broken, and there was graffiti covering most of the old sign. Beneath that, what must have once been the box office had long since been turned into glass doors that had been boarded over and chained shut for most of the past few decades.

After the theater had closed back in the eighties, the building had become a department store for a while, and when that closed, a church had met there for several years, and occasionally it had been used as a Halloween shop or another pop-up shop of some kind. But mostly it had sat empty, to Janet's memory. What must have once been a beautiful building had become sad and dilapidated, and Janet was happy that Sam had bought it and was turning it back into something useful again.

As Janet and Debbie approached the theater, Greg went ahead to open the doors and usher them in. "You'll need to wear hard hats, since this is an active construction site," he said, handing one to each of them. Janet and Debbie took the hats and slipped them on.

"Wow," Janet said as they stepped inside. Floodlights suspended on wires lit up the space. Wallpaper hung off the plaster walls in sheets, and the walls themselves were water-stained and covered in grime. The industrial carpet underfoot felt sticky and smelled like must. The ceiling soared above them, and behind the layers of paint and grime and dust, she could see that the carved woodwork was beautiful. Ahead was a space that no doubt had been the concession stand, though now it held only a table saw, sawhorses, toolboxes, and other construction equipment. A hallway blocked by floor-to-ceiling plastic sheeting branched off on both sides of the concession stand.

Sam arrived as they were taking in the scene. "This was the lobby, obviously," he said.

"You can see that it was beautiful once." Debbie gazed up at the ceiling. "That must be where the chandelier hung?"

"Yes," Sam said. He gestured them forward. "You already saw it on the film, but I've got a picture of what it used to look like here. You might be able to see it better. Come look."

They crossed the lobby. Sam had taped historical photos of the theater to one of the side walls. The first photo showed the lobby, and even in the grainy black-and-white shot, it was clear this space had once been grand. The soaring ceiling had intricately carved woodwork and an enormous cut-glass chandelier. The concession stand was made of carved wood and curved glass with a mirrored backsplash. The date *1942* was etched into the corner of the photo.

"It's so hard to believe there was a place like this in Dennison," Debbie said.

"It was the golden age of Hollywood," Sam said. "Going to the theater to see the stars was an event."

"This is incredible." Janet leaned forward and looked at the next photo, which showed the front of the building as it had been. The lit marquee advertised a showing of *Casablanca,* and the brick facade was studded with posters for other movies. Janet squinted and made out the poster for *Outlaw,* and another for *For Whom the Bell Tolls.* There was a photo that showed workmen in overalls and hard hats pounding nails into the wall of what must have been an auditorium, judging by the giant screen at the front of the room. *1946* was etched into the corner of that picture.

Beside that photo was another shot, this one showing the interior of the theater itself. The picture was taken from the back of the auditorium, and at the front was a large screen flanked by heavy velvet curtains. Rows of adjoining velvet-covered seats faced the screen, which showed a black-and-white film Janet didn't recognize.

"Are you planning to restore this place to look like this?" Debbie asked, turning back around.

"As close as I can get it," Sam said. He smiled, and the corners of his eyes crinkled. "The plan is to show World War II-era movies, as well as more modern movies set during the war. So *Casablanca* and *Citizen Kane,* but also things like *Dunkirk, Saving Private Ryan, Courage Under Fire,* that kind of thing. Since I'll be hearkening back to the golden age of Hollywood, the plan is to try to recreate the experience as much as I can."

"That sounds wonderful," Janet said. She would love to come here to see a film once the theater was restored.

"Where were the canisters hidden?" Debbie asked, turning around to take in the once-grand room again.

"This way." Sam gestured for them to follow and led them to the left hallway, toward an area that was draped off with plastic. "Bathrooms are on either side of the concession stand," he said as they walked past a metal door. "They're pretty grim but still technically functional."

"'Technically functional' is not how any bathroom I want to use would be described," Debbie said.

"What's that?" Janet pointed at a wooden door that hung off its hinges just to the right of the bathroom door.

"Behind that door is what I'm using as my office for now," Sam said.

"Seems very secure," Janet said, smiling.

Sam laughed. "Now you see why I wanted to keep the film somewhere else. The whole place is under video surveillance, but I just don't feel good about leaving it here unless it can be secured."

As they neared the draped plastic, Greg stepped forward and pushed it aside, holding it open as they all stepped through. He turned on his phone's flashlight and led them forward, and Janet followed tentatively. There were no windows back here, and there were no lights until Greg connected an extension cord to something that she guessed was a portable generator. "We have to redo the electrical, so excuse the darkness," Greg said.

Floodlights blinked on, lighting up the cavernous space.

"Turns out the wiring from the 1930s isn't up to code, if you can believe it," Sam said with a laugh.

"Wow," Janet said. She'd thought the lobby was a mess, but behind the plastic were partially demolished walls and bare wall frames. Everything was coated in a thick layer of fine white powder. "This is quite a project."

"Exactly the way I like it." Greg grinned.

"This started out as one big auditorium," Sam said. "In 1946, they divided it up and made two theaters out of it, so there were two screens. Remember that photo with the workmen? They had to make the seats smaller but could fit more people in altogether. So this was one side"—he indicated the left side of the space—"and this was the other." He pointed to the right. The remains of a wall stood between the two areas. "But when this was used as a department store, they opened up doorways in the wall and used these for men's and women's clothes. I think the church closed those openings back up and used one side for church and the other for classrooms, which is why you can see that there were more interior walls over here." He gestured to the right side, though Janet honestly couldn't tell where the walls had been in all the mess.

"I was working up here," Greg said, indicating the back wall of the left auditorium. It was little more than lath with some grayish plaster attached in sections at this point.

"They don't build walls like that anymore," Debbie said, nodding at the lath.

"They don't," Greg agreed. "Good thing too. As cool as it looks, today's materials are much more efficient."

"This wall was damaged by a pipe that burst a decade or so ago," Sam said. "So Greg was pulling it down."

"I discovered that the far side of the wall is plaster and lath, but this side was done in drywall, which was easy to pull off," Greg said. "Once I got going, I was able to open up the wall pretty quickly."

Janet could see plaster leaking through the cracks in between the lath on the far side of the wall, and nail holes in the framing pieces where the drywall had been affixed on this side.

"Fortunately most of the plaster and lath is in good shape, so we left that. But when I pulled off the last piece of drywall, over here"—he gestured to the bottom left section of the wall—"the film canisters came tumbling out."

Janet stepped forward and bent down, examining the space. It would have been very narrow, just barely wide enough for the thin film canister to sit once the drywall was in place.

"But how did they get in there?" Debbie asked, leaning forward to get a better view.

"That is the question, isn't it?" Greg said. "I don't know. I mean, obviously someone put up the drywall with it there, but I can't tell you how or why."

"What's on the other side of this wall?" Janet asked.

"The back of the concession stand," Sam said.

"Huh." Janet tried to picture it. "So is this wall from the 1946 renovation, or from before?"

"The lath and plaster side is earlier," Greg said. "I would guess that's original to the building. But with lumber being restricted during the war, drywall became much more common in the forties, so I imagine the drywall side was done as part of the 1946 renovation."

"Fascinating." Janet tried to think of some explanation for how the film had ended up there, but couldn't. There was really only one logical answer—whoever had stolen it had hidden it there, knowing it probably wouldn't be found for a very long time. That someone must have had direct access to the theater, especially the sections that were under construction in 1946.

"You all are welcome to look around longer," Greg said, "but I'm going to get back to work."

"In that case, we'll get out of your way," Debbie said. She leaned in and gave him a kiss on the cheek.

"I'll call you later," he promised.

"Thank you so much for showing us this space," Janet said. "And for showing us the film."

"Seriously. This day took a totally unexpected turn, and it's awesome," Debbie said. "Let us know if you find anything else cool in there."

"I will." Greg laughed.

Sam walked them out, back through the plastic sheeting and the broken-down lobby. The whole place had a sense of decayed grandeur that struck something in Janet.

"It's going to be beautiful when it's done," Debbie said.

"I sure hope so." Sam smiled and let them out the front door. Once they'd taken off their hard hats and stepped out onto the sidewalk, Janet turned and looked up at the front of the old theater. The marquee was broken and dilapidated, but in her mind, she could picture it the way it had appeared in the photo. Maybe someday soon it would look like that again.

"I guess we should head back," Debbie said. But Janet heard the hesitation in her voice.

"Yeah, probably." Janet had her project she'd planned to work on this afternoon. But after what had just happened, she wasn't itching to get back the way she normally would be. Instead, she was considering a stop before she headed home. "I was thinking maybe we should go to the library first."

"The library?" Debbie asked. She cocked an eyebrow.

"After seeing that footage, I think I want to learn more about the theft. Like, how did it go missing, and when? That kind of thing. We know it was stolen, but that's all I've heard about it. I wondered if the newspapers from that time would be able to shed some light on it. If you don't want to go, I can take you back to the café before I head over to the library, but—"

"That's a great idea," Debbie said. "I'm curious as well. Let's do it."

CHAPTER FOUR

The library was only a few blocks away, but on this raw winter day, they decided to drive over in Janet's car. They found a parking spot and walked into the two-story brick building. The sweet familiar scent of paper and glue hung in the air, and though a display of spring-themed picture books arranged on a front table felt distinctly aspirational today, Janet was glad to see them.

"Hello there!" Ellie Cartwright, the head librarian, called from the front desk. "Hi, Janet, Debbie. How are you both doing?"

"Just fine," Debbie said.

"We're here to look through some old newspapers," Janet said.

"How old are we talking?" Ellie adjusted a pin in the hair bun on top of her head.

"From the 1940s," Debbie said.

"Pretty old, then. You'll need to look at the *Evening Chronicle*, in that case."

Janet nodded. The current local newspaper, the *Gazette*—run by Sam Watson's brother Jim—started up sometime after the *Evening Chronicle* folded in 1981. "That's all on microfiche, isn't it?" Janet had looked through old editions of the paper at some point last year, and while she found newer digital retrieval systems more convenient, there was something she loved about seeing the old papers laid out in their original format.

"That's right. You remember where it is?"

"The boxes are in the filing cabinets against the wall, unless they've moved." Debbie pointed toward the far wall, next to the row of research terminals.

"They should be arranged by year, but let me know if something is missing," Ellie said. "The microfiche machine is on the far side of the cabinets."

"Thanks so much." Janet and Debbie walked across the hardwood floor to the cabinets. Long white drawers were labeled with the names of various publications and years. Janet narrowed in on the drawers for the *Evening Chronicle* and opened the one labeled *1938-1946*. Inside were dozens of boxes of microfiche sheets, each labeled with a month and year.

"Do we know what month Clark Gable was in town?" she asked.

"The first film canister was labeled September 1944," Debbie said.

"Perfect." She scooped up the boxes for September and October 1944 and gently pushed the drawer closed. Debbie walked over to the viewing machine and pressed the button on the side to turn it on. The screen filled with the familiar yellow-brown glow.

"This reminds me so much of college," Debbie said, sliding the first rectangular sheet of film into the reader. The screen filled with blurry black-and-white type over the golden background. Debbie twisted a knob to adjust the focus, and the front page of the September 1 issue of the *Evening Chronicle* appeared on the screen. "I spent so many nights at the library doing this."

"I'm pretty sure Tiffany has never used microfiche," Janet said. "She does so much of her research on her phone. College has changed a lot since our day."

"Pretty much everything has," Debbie said with a laugh. "Let's see. A theft like this would probably have been front-page news in a local paper, don't you think?" She pointed up at the top left corner, where the front page of the paper was positioned on the screen.

Dewey turns up heat on Roosevelt, read the headline. Below that were other articles: More Remains Identified in Normandy. D-Day had happened in June of 1944, so that was no doubt what this article was referencing. Football Season Starts with a Bang for State.

"I'm sure it would be, but just in case, let's skim the headlines on each of the pages," Janet said, and Debbie nodded.

The type was small and hard to read, but they scanned the pages quickly and decided there was no mention of Clark Gable in this issue. Debbie pulled out the sheet and replaced it with the film for September 2. They read through the headlines here, and again, decided it didn't have what they were looking for. Janet had to force herself to focus on the headlines to not get distracted by all the ads and the local pieces in the paper. Having the whole issue laid out in its original format meant they got to see the issue just as the original readers would have.

They moved pretty quickly through the cards for the first half of September, and on September 19, they found their first mention of Clark Gable's visit to town. Hollywood Star Clark Gable Visits Area to Make Movie, the headline read.

"Can you make that type bigger?" Janet asked, and when Debbie zoomed in, they both squinted at the screen to read the article.

Academy award-winning actor Clark Gable arrived in Dennison yesterday, where he was greeted by adoring fans. Gable, who won the Oscar for Best Actor in It Happened One Night *in 1934, joined the army in 1942 after the death of his wife Carole Lombard, and spent the last two years overseas in active military duty. While he was stationed in England, he directed and starred in a film called* Combat America, *which the star claims will give everyday Americans a glimpse into the struggles of life in the military. That film has yet to be released, but Gable is already at work on his next project, which he says focuses on the war effort on the home front.*

Asked how long he would be in town, Gable responded, "As long as it takes." In addition to shooting scenes in Ohio for the upcoming film, the actor says he has plans to document the war effort in other parts of the country, including around New London, Connecticut, the submarine capital of the world, and Southern California, where many ships carrying soldiers headed for the Pacific depart.

The town of Dennison gave the star a warm welcome, with Mayor Louis Humphreys sending a fruit basket to the star's room at the Del Mar on behalf of the people of Dennison.

"I guess it was big news when he showed up," Debbie said.

"It's not every day a major Hollywood celebrity comes to Dennison," Janet said. "It makes sense that people paid attention. Let's see what else it says."

There were several follow-up articles over the next few days. The paper reported on where Gable had been seen filming, which restaurants he ate at, and which movies he went to see at the local theater.

"It appears he took the theater owner up on his offer of free tickets," Debbie said.

"Considering the film was discovered in the theater, it's worth noting that Gable went there while he was in town," Janet said.

"Do you think that could be connected somehow?"

"I'm not sure," Janet said. "If the film ended up in the wall when they renovated two years after he was here, I don't see how it could be connected, but maybe it is and we just don't see it yet."

"It seems like he went several times," Debbie said. "It's mentioned in a couple of the articles. I guess there probably wasn't a lot to do here in Dennison. Not for someone who was used to living the high life in Hollywood, anyway."

"Maybe he just really liked movies," Janet said. "Like a writer who spends their spare time reading other authors' books."

"That's possible," Debbie said. "In any case, at least we know that he went to the movie theater. Though, honestly, I'm not sure how that helps us."

Janet skimmed the next slide Debbie loaded. "When did the theft actually happen?" Janet asked.

"I don't know," Debbie said. "Let's keep looking."

They read through the pages for September 25, 26, 27, and 28, but it wasn't until the September 29 paper that the theft was mentioned.

Movie Footage Stolen from Clark Gable's Hotel Room

Police received a call at 10:32 p.m. reporting the loss of the footage shot by Hollywood star Clark Gable. Gable, who has been staying in Dennison while shooting scenes for his upcoming documentary about the war effort on the home front, returned from the Sunshine Cinemas to find the film, which he'd kept on the desk in his hotel room, missing.

"We are disheartened to hear about the missing film," said Bernard Williams, the manager on duty at the time of the film's disappearance. "We are fully cooperating with the police and will do whatever we can to make sure this matter is resolved successfully and the film is returned." He added that the Del Mar has top-notch security and is a safe and pleasant destination.

According to those familiar with the situation, Gable had been staying in the same room since he checked in to the hotel nearly two weeks ago, and he had expensive camera equipment with him in his room which was not taken. A maid at the hotel, who refused to give her name, said the film had been left out in plain sight inside the hotel room for several days.

"We are working with Mr. Gable to explore every possibility as to what happened to the film," said Police Chief Frank Hannigan. "We will not rest until that film is returned to its proper owner."

The following day's newspaper had a similar story.

HOLLYWOOD STAR'S FILM REMAINS UNACCOUNTED FOR

Rolls of film that were stolen from movie star Clark Gable's hotel room have not been recovered, according to Dennison police, though Police Chief Frank Hannigan maintains that the force is investigating all leads and will stop at nothing to make sure the thief is caught and the film returned.

The Hollywood star's film is not the first thing to have gone missing from the Del Mar in recent months, according to a source with knowledge of the hotel's history. The source reports that jewelry and other valuable items have been discovered missing by half a dozen guests in recent months, and the hotel management has not been able to recover the missing items. Asked to comment on the accusation, management at the hotel maintained that guests had misplaced their items and denied any wrongdoing.

"Well, that seems shady," Debbie said. "It sounds like this hotel wasn't a 'safe and pleasant destination' after all."

"That does indeed sound suspicious," Janet said. "One or two guests misplacing their items, maybe. But half a dozen? How does that happen?"

"It sounds like someone at the hotel was probably behind those thefts," Debbie agreed. "Which makes it likely they had something to do with the missing film too."

"Let's keep reading and see if they have anything more," Janet said.

Suspects Questioned in Gable Film Theft;
No Answers Yet

Dennison Police are not commenting on how many suspects have been interviewed in the disappearance of the film from star Clark Gable's hotel room.

Police Chief Hannigan said, "We are working to put together a picture of the events that night," and refused to comment further.

Meanwhile, rumors have been flying about the alleged altercation between the Hollywood star and the management of the hotel the day before the theft was reported. According to witnesses, the manager of the hotel, Bernard Williams, confronted the star in the lobby to demand payment for his stay. Gable promised his bill would be settled fairly, and Williams was overheard to say that Gable would be sorry if payment was not made swiftly.

"I would have thought the manager would pull Clark aside to ask about his bill, but he just confronted him out in the open in the lobby," said Meredith DiSalvo, another guest at the hotel.

Williams has denied having anything to do with the disappearance of the film and would neither confirm nor deny that he has been interviewed by the police several times.

Williams reported to the police that a young woman was found wandering in the hallway outside the room where Gable was staying the night the film went missing. He refused to name her publicly but mentioned that the police had been in touch with her and were investigating.

"That sounds decidedly fishy," Debbie said. "The hotel manager tells him to pay his bill or else, and then the film goes missing?"

"But why hadn't he paid his bill?" Janet asked. "Wouldn't a big star like Clark Gable have no trouble paying for his hotel room?"

"I don't know," Debbie said. "And even if he was having money trouble, why would the manager confront him in the lobby in front of everyone? Why not do it discreetly, behind closed doors?"

"It sure sounds like something strange was going on at the hotel," Janet said. "What about the woman found wandering the halls?"

"I don't know. The way the article reads, it almost sounds like he threw that out there to take suspicion off the hotel employees."

"You think there wasn't really a woman?"

"I have no idea. Maybe there was. But who was she, and why wouldn't he name her?"

"Something strange indeed," Janet said. "Maybe the next few days' papers will tell us more."

The October 2 edition didn't report much of an update.

Police Still Searching For Missing Film

Dennison police are still searching for clues as to the whereabouts of footage stolen from the hotel room of Hollywood star Clark Gable. Police Chief Hannigan told reporters, "We are looking into every clue and will not rest until we find the missing film."

When asked about the people who have been interviewed by the police so far, Hannigan refused to comment. He would not disclose the name of a young woman rumored to have been discovered in the hallway outside the star's room while he was out because she is a minor.

After the news of the theft broke, many of Gable's supporters arrived in Dennison.

Frederick Hallman, who identified himself as a producer from the film studio where Gable is under contract, told reporters, "We are heartbroken to hear of this heinous crime, and we stand behind Clark Gable. We will find that film."

Other supporters who have arrived in Dennison include Gable's manager Tony Friese and agent Mark Justino.

"That one reads like the reporter had a deadline but no actual news to report," Debbie said.

Janet had to agree, except for one thing. "The woman in the hallway was a minor. You don't think it was—"

"There's no reason to assume it was the waitress in the diner," Debbie said.

"But it could have been. And the fact that your mind went right there tells me you were thinking the same thing."

"Sure, it could have been. But it could have been anyone. What would she have been doing in the hallway outside his room?"

"Who knows? I'm just saying, it's a possibility." Janet thought for a moment. "You know what else strikes me?"

"What?"

"They all keep going on about what a tragedy it is that these film rolls were lost. But it's not all that much footage. Sure, it took some time, and some of the interviews with people like the soldier who were just coming through town would be hard to recreate, but most of the people he interviewed lived here. He could just redo the interviews if he wanted to. So why is this such a big deal?"

"I mean, he's a big star. It is a big deal."

"Yes, but if he was passionate about this project, why didn't he get some more rolls of film and redo the interviews? Why abandon the project altogether?"

"I don't know," Debbie said. "It's a good question. Maybe his heart just wasn't in it. He was mourning his wife, and people don't always act rationally in the throes of grief. Maybe another project came up. It's hard to say."

"It's just a bit strange."

"Maybe." Debbie shrugged. "Let's keep reading."

There wasn't a lot revealed in the papers that followed.

GABLE LEAVES TOWN, DISILLUSIONED BY FRUITLESS SEARCH

INVESTIGATORS NOT GIVING UP IN GABLE THEFT CASE

STILL NO SIGN OF GABLE'S MISSING FOOTAGE

"It kind of falls off after that," Debbie said. She slipped in the next microfiche slide and scanned it, then another. They methodically went through the next several weeks of newspapers. "Here's one two months later," she said after a while. "It's just basically saying that they haven't learned anything."

"There's got to be more. Didn't Kim say the theft was national news?"

"Yes. Do you want to see where else the story was reported?"

"We might as well, right?"

"Let's go to the computers," Debbie said. "We'll see what we can find in the database."

They moved to one of the computer terminals and opened the program that searched newspapers from across the country. Janet narrowed their search parameters, looking for articles in 1944 that contained the phrases *Clark Gable* and *theft* or *stolen*. Sure enough, they found articles in the *New York Times*, the *Los Angeles Times*, and the *Chicago Tribune,* among others. They read all the articles, but none of them revealed information they didn't already have.

"Okay," Janet said. "So what do we know?"

Debbie pulled a notebook and pen out of her purse and flipped to a fresh page. "We know the film footage was stored in Clark Gable's hotel room and that things had gone missing from hotel rooms at the Del Mar before that."

"I wonder why something as valuable as his next film project wasn't kept in a safe at the hotel," Janet said.

"Maybe they didn't have safes in every hotel room back then," Debbie replied. "But surely the hotel had a safe guests could use or a way to secure valuables."

"Maybe Clark didn't think he needed it. Maybe he thought it was safe enough in his room. Dennison, Ohio, isn't exactly a hot spot for crime. It probably seemed secure enough. The only people who had access to the room were hotel staff."

"Which brings us to the hotel staff," Debbie said. "We have the manager confronting Gable in the lobby over payment for the room. So I would say he's on the suspect list." She scribbled *hotel manager* on the notebook in front of her.

"For sure," Janet said. "I'd love to know more about that. Why didn't Clark Gable pay his hotel bill? What was going on there?"

"That's definitely worth trying to learn more about," Debbie said. "Bernard Williams is the same guy who was interviewed in the footage we saw. The staff appeared friendly enough then, but I guess we don't know when in his stay that segment was recorded."

Janet pulled up the video on her phone and played back that segment. "He sure doesn't seem upset or like he's threatened Gable recently," she said after watching the video again.

"Well, in any case, we should find out more about him," Debbie said.

"And we should also check into whoever had access to the key. I imagine there weren't huge numbers of people who would have been able to get it," Janet said. "But a hotel maid would."

Debbie wrote *Maid?* on the notebook page.

"Or maybe whoever it was had been let in by Clark," Janet said.

"What do you mean?"

"Just looking at all the possibilities. Either someone snuck in while he was out and took the footage, or he let someone into the room and they took it."

"The newspaper said he was at the theater watching a movie when the film was stolen. Do you think he let someone into his room, left, and they ran off with it while he was gone? Wouldn't he have told the police, if that was the case?"

"I don't know," Janet said. "But there's no mention in any of the newspaper reports of anyone staying with Gable in his hotel room. Again, that would have come up."

"And of course we have to consider that someone at the theater might have had something to do with it, considering where the film was found. The police may not have even known the theater was of interest here, since they clearly didn't know that's where the footage ended up."

"Given that's where Gable was at the time of the theft, I'm sure they spoke to people at the theater if they thought there was any reason to," Janet said. "If only to check that he was really there. But obviously no one saw what happened with the film or how it ended up there."

"How it ended up behind a wall at the theater," Debbie said. "A wall that wasn't built until two years *after* the film was stolen. If the film had been found dumped in a trash can or something, anyone could have done it, but since it was hidden behind a wall—that suggests someone who had good access to the place, and someone who was around two years later."

She wrote *theater person* on the list.

"But the person who stole it and the person who hid it could be different," Janet pointed out. "So maybe we have two lists of suspects. Who stole the film, and who hid it in the wall in 1946?"

"And where was it in between?" Debbie said. "I think it's fair to say someone with a lot of access to the theater was involved in hiding it. So for that part of the mystery, at least, it would be good if we could find someone who worked at the theater." She tapped her pen against the table. "What was the name of that guy Gable interviewed in the footage? The guy who owned the theater?"

"Stanley Hersey."

"Good memory."

Janet shook her head. "Not really. I just know that because my dad was friends with his son Max growing up. My parents still see Max a few times a year. My dad used to talk about how awesome it was to have a friend whose parents owned the local movie theater."

"Would Max's parents have owned it in 1944?" Debbie asked. "That was before your parents were born, right?"

"That's a good point." Janet's dad hadn't been born until 1953, and she thought Max was probably around the same age. "I can ask my dad about that."

"Great. Now, what about the film studio executive quoted in that article?" Debbie asked. "What do we think of him?"

"I don't know," Janet said. "There's not a lot to go on there. It sounds like he supported his big star, which makes sense."

"But why did he come all the way out to Dennison to do that?"

"To encourage him?" Janet repeated.

"Maybe." Debbie wrote *Film Studio Exec Frederick Hallman* down on her list anyway. "I want to find out more about him."

"Was he even in town when the film went missing, though? Or did he come out afterward to support Gable and the studio's movie?" Janet was pretty sure Debbie was reaching on this one.

"Was Gable making the film for the studio? I didn't see that mentioned anywhere."

"Why wouldn't he be? And if that's the case, of course the executive would be invested in what happened to the missing footage."

"I don't know. I still think he's worth looking into more," Debbie said.

"If you say so." Janet thought there were much more plausible suspects on the list already, but if Debbie wanted to add him, she wasn't going to stop her.

"Anyone else?"

"I think that's a pretty good start," Janet said. She and Debbie had never actually agreed that they were going to look into the theft more, or try to figure out how the film ended up behind the wall of the theater, but at some point during the afternoon it had just become clear that they were. "I wonder how we can learn more about the people on this list."

"Janet? Debbie?" They both turned and found Ellie Cartwright standing behind them. "The library is closing in five minutes, I'm afraid."

The librarian's tone was apologetic, but it was clear that she needed them to pack it in. Janet looked at her watch. Goodness. It was almost five. She'd been so absorbed in research that she had totally missed how late it had gotten.

"We'll clean this all up," Janet said. "Thank you for letting us know."

As Ellie went off to tell other patrons about the looming deadline, Debbie said, "I'm going to see if they have any books about Clark Gable here. Or anything else that might be useful." She grabbed her purse and dashed off toward the stacks. Janet logged off the computer, turned off the microfiche machine, repacked the slides neatly in the boxes, and replaced them in the drawers. Then she picked up her purse and headed to the front of the library, where Debbie was already waiting in line at the checkout desk.

"Find something?"

Debbie held up a biography of Clark Gable. The cover featured the star with his best smoldering gaze.

"Nice. But will you have time to read that while you're planning a wedding?"

"There is always time for a good book."

Janet couldn't argue with that. After Debbie had checked out the book, they walked to Janet's car and she drove back to the café, where Debbie's car was still parked. It had only been a few hours ago that Greg had called and said he'd found the film, and that had set this whole thing in motion. Before that, Janet hadn't thought about Clark Gable in years. Now the star and his stolen film were all she could think about.

She should head home and get started on dinner. Ian would be home soon, and while he never expected she would have dinner on the table, she liked to make food she knew he'd like.

Still, she had time to make one stop. It was hardly out of the way. Besides, Ian couldn't object to Janet stopping by to see her parents.

And maybe while she was there Dad could tell her something about the old theater owner.

CHAPTER FIVE

*J*anet drove up in front of her parents' place a few minutes later. The Hills' home was on a street lined with bungalows and tall trees whose branches arched over the road. Janet had grown up in a cute blue house with a covered front porch where Janet's mom, a retired book editor, spent a lot of time reading in good weather.

Janet stepped inside and found her mom bent over a cutting board, slicing baby potatoes in half. Her gray hair was pulled back in a ponytail, and she wore a flowered apron over her Dennison High sweatshirt. The smell of onions and some kind of roasting meat filled the kitchen. Dad was seated in the recliner in the living room, reading a biography of Winston Churchill. A lamp on the table next to him cast a warm glow around him. He looked up and smiled at Janet.

"Hi, Janet. Good to see you." Mom used the side of her knife to scoop up the potatoes she'd sliced and set them in a roasting pan. She narrowed her eyes, and Janet saw that she was worried. Janet didn't usually stop in at this time of day. "Is everything all right?"

"Everything is fine," Janet said. "I just was hoping to talk to Dad for a minute if he's free."

"Well, you'd be preventing me from learning how this war turns out," Dad said, placing a bookmark in his book.

"Spoiler alert: the Allies win," Janet said.

"Now you've done it." Dad laughed and closed the book, setting it on the table next to him. He had a plaid wool blanket Janet and Ian had brought back from a trip to Scotland on his lap. He adjusted it as he turned to her. "So what's up?"

"Didn't you have a friend whose parents owned the movie theater when you were a kid?"

Dad laughed again. "I don't know what I expected you to say, but it wasn't that."

"It's not as random as it sounds, I promise. Did you hear that Jim Watson's brother Sam moved back to town and plans to reopen the old movie theater?"

"I had heard that," Mom called from the kitchen. "It's good to see Sammy home again, though I don't know if the theater is going to work out for him. Doesn't everyone stream movies at home these days?"

"I think his idea is to show World War II films. I hear there are some people around here who like movies about that time in history." She winked at Dad. "Greg is working on the renovation, and today when he was knocking down a wall he found something strange." Janet told them about the film canisters and their contents.

Mom set her knife on the counter. "Oh wow. I'd heard about Clark Gable's visit to town. It was quite a big deal around here, I guess. Mom and Dad talked about it sometimes. So I'd heard about the stolen footage, but I guess I thought it was lost for good."

"Apparently it was in the theater the whole time," Janet said, shrugging. "No one knows how it got there."

"Well, *someone* knows how it got there," Dad said.

"Right." Dad's logical mind was, of course, correct. "But that person, whoever it is, is probably long gone. Anyway, Debbie and I were talking about it, and I remembered your friend Max—didn't you say his father owned the movie theater when you were kids?"

"He did indeed," Dad said. "It was the best."

"Your father still complains whenever he has to pay full price for a movie," Mom said.

"Max's parents were older," Dad said. "It was pretty clear he was a late-in-life surprise for them. It's not that they didn't pay attention to him. It was more that they had their hands full, so Max basically had the run of the theater."

"I see you chose your friend strategically," Janet said. "Nicely done."

"I didn't know what his parents did when we started playing together on the kindergarten playground. His dad could have been something boring, like a CPA, for all I knew." A retired CPA, Dad grinned at his own joke. "But I got lucky. Max's parents owned the theater, and we basically just hung out there most Saturdays while his parents worked. We'd watch whatever movie was playing, and we got as much free popcorn as we wanted, and it was awesome. Sometimes we got lucky and it was a double feature, or sometimes we'd pop in and out of the two auditoriums and see bits of both movies. Occasionally we were known to launch popcorn from the back row or startle couples getting a little too cozy. We had a lot of fun, that's for sure."

It was funny to think of her dad running around the theater as a kid. And Max Hersey—a retired judge they saw several times a year—was always so reserved. She couldn't imagine the two of them wreaking havoc on the small-town theater.

"I don't know, they probably wouldn't allow kids to just roam all around the theater these days, but back then, it felt like a very safe place to be," Dad said. "Plus, all the other kids were jealous."

"That's what's important," Mom added.

"Do you know if Max's parents owned the theater in 1944?"

"I don't know," Dad said. "I imagine they did, because I never heard of anyone else owning it, but that was before my time, so I can't say for sure."

"Would Max know?"

"Probably." Dad paused. "Wait. Do you think his parents *knew* about the Clark Gable film being at the theater?"

"I don't know," Janet said. "But given that's where it turned up, it seems like it's probably worth asking the question."

"Max will help you if he can," Dad said. "Do you have his number?"

"No, I don't think so."

"Let me get it for you." Dad pressed the lever to lower the footrest of his recliner, and then he pushed himself up and lumbered into the kitchen. His phone was charging on the counter. He forwarded the contact card to Janet. "Just sent it to you."

Janet's phone dinged in her purse. "Sounds like I just got it."

"I'll text him to let him know you'll be getting in touch," Dad said. He did some more tapping on his screen and then put it back on the counter.

"Thank you." Janet turned to Mom. "Is there anything I can help you with?"

"I don't think so. I just need to get these potatoes in the oven, and then I'm going to get off my feet for a few minutes." Mom opened the oven door, set the dish inside, and then straightened up. "Would you like to stay for dinner?"

"No, thank you. I need to get home and get our dinner started. Ian will be home any minute. But thank you for the invite, and thank you for the contact info for Max."

"It would be so neat to get answers after all this time," Mom said. "I hope he's able to help."

"Me too."

Ian was just walking in the door when Janet pulled into the driveway. After he gave her a kiss on the cheek, he took Laddie out for a walk while she quickly put together chicken quesadillas. While she worked, she called Max Hersey. He picked up quickly.

"Janet! It's good to hear from you," he said, his voice warm. Max had always been kind to her, and he had doted on Tiffany when she was younger. "How's your little girl?"

"Not so little anymore. She's almost done with her second year of college," Janet said.

"That's impossible," Max said. "Tell her to stop growing up."

"I've tried," Janet said. "It isn't working, though."

Janet explained what had happened at the theater and why she was calling, and Max let out a low whistle.

"Are you serious? You're sure it's the missing Clark Gable film?"

"Pretty sure," Janet said. "And I wondered if your parents owned the theater back in 1944."

"They did indeed," Max said. "They opened it in 1939 and had it until it closed in 1985. It was long past time for them to retire by then, but they just loved it so much. I can promise you my parents didn't know anything about that film being in the theater. They talked about it a lot, how Clark Gable had come into their theater just about every night while he was in here. It was a big deal, having a big Hollywood star in town, and the fact that he spent so much time at the theater was something they were very proud of. They were more disappointed than anybody when the film went missing and Gable left town without finishing the movie. They talked about it sometimes, but they never mentioned anything about the film being in the theater."

"Is there any chance they knew and just...never said anything?"

"I mean..." He let his voice trail off. "I don't think so. I just don't see how." He was quiet for a moment. "But I'll tell you what. I have a ton of stuff from the old theater in the attic. When the place finally closed, they carted off a bunch of things from over the decades, and I've never had the stomach to go through it and toss things out."

"Really?" Janet couldn't believe items from the theater in the forties and fifties were still lying around in storage nearby.

"It's mostly old movie posters, ticket machines, some of the old velvet chairs, that kind of thing. A lot of out-of-date technology. But there are also boxes and boxes of records from the office in there somewhere. If you want, I could go through it and see if there's anything in any of the records to indicate they knew something?"

"Would you?"

"How about I start, and you can come over to talk to me about whatever I find?"

"Are you kidding? I would love that." Max lived in Steubenville, near the Pennsylvania border.

"Great. When is good?"

"Whenever works for you."

He laughed. "I'm retired. Anytime is good for me. But we're leaving for Europe on Saturday, so sooner is probably better. How about tomorrow?"

"I could be there by about three," Janet said.

"Wait—I've got my pickleball lesson at three. Could you do any later? Maybe five or so?"

"Sure." She could make that work. "Would it be okay if I brought Debbie?"

"Of course. How's Debbie doing?"

"Great. She just got engaged, actually. To the contractor who found the film."

"That's great news. Tell her to come along too. I'll see you both then."

"That sounds good."

Janet hung up, her heart hopeful. Maybe by this time tomorrow they'd have some answers.

Once the kitchen was clean and Ian was settled in front of the television, Janet decided to take a few minutes and get to work on her project. For months, she'd been working in spurts on gathering a collection of family recipes and the recipes they used at the Whistle Stop Café. She'd recently realized she could give a copy to Debbie as a wedding present. She'd been saving recipes here and there when she found something she thought Debbie would like, but she still had more to gather. She had worked on the layout for some pages, but she'd also seen sites online that helped people create a bound book. There was still work to do before she decided how to put it together.

She gathered the pictures of the recipes she'd taken that day. The recipe for the corn bread they served at the café was stained and much-used, but she had the original on her computer. The fried chicken recipe was somewhere in her files too. There wasn't really a recipe for the turkey club their customers loved so much, but Janet typed up the ingredients she always made sure to include.

Janet would also need to include the recipes for the baked goods she made fresh each morning for the café. Speaking of which… She glanced at the clock. It was getting late. She needed to get to bed. She still had a lot more work to do, but the alarm went off early. She'd worry about this tomorrow.

CHAPTER SIX

anet was just taking the blueberry crumble muffins out of the
oven when she heard Debbie walk into the café Tuesday morning. Janet set the muffins on a rack to cool and went out to say hello.

"Did you know that Clark Gable was baptized in Dennison?"
Debbie asked, peeling off her heavy coat as she stepped inside.

"A very good morning to you as well," Janet said.

"Good morning. And did you know that?"

"I did not," Janet said. "Why? I thought he was from Cadiz."

"He was. Not the one in Spain, the one just down the road."

"I had gathered that." The town of Cadiz, about twenty miles
from Dennison, was less famous than its Spanish counterpart.

"He was born in 1901. His dad William was an oil well driller,
and his mom's name was Adeline. Addie. He was Protestant, and
she was Catholic. When he was six months old, Addie brought him
to Dennison and had him secretly baptized at the Catholic church
here in town." As she spoke, Debbie crossed into the kitchen and
stashed her bag and coat in the office.

"You must have enjoyed that book you got at the library." Janet
took the tray of scones she'd set on the counter earlier and arranged
them on the display shelf.

"It's an entertaining read," Debbie said. "Though I doubt I would have cared all that much if it wasn't for that film."

"I'm sure you're right," Janet said. "But since we did find it, what else did you learn?"

"His mother died when he was ten months old."

"That's sad."

"It seems she hadn't been well for a while. His father remarried, and when Clark was sixteen, his father moved the family to Palmyra, near Akron."

"What about the stepmother? Was she okay?"

"She treated treat Clark well, from what I can tell. When he was seventeen, he got a job at a tire company then got the acting bug and began working for traveling theater companies before eventually moving to Hollywood. He got some roles in a few films, got married a few times—"

"As one does."

"I'm skipping a lot or this will take all day. In 1934, he starred in *It Happened One Night*, for which he won the Academy Award for Best Actor. His third wife was actress Carole Lombard, and by all accounts they were very happy together."

As she talked, Debbie took cash out of the safe and set up the register, and Janet brought the rest of the baked goods out of the kitchen and set them up behind the glass display case.

"Uh-oh. I read about her at the museum. Didn't she—"

"Lombard was killed in a plane crash in 1942. She had just finished her fifty-seventh movie and had been on a war bond selling tour, helping to raise money for the war effort."

"That's tragic."

"It affected Clark deeply, as you might imagine. A few months later, in August 1942, he joined the army."

"I'm surprised he just left it all behind. Not too many would give up stardom and riches to fight in the military today."

"As you saw at the museum, he wasn't the only one," Debbie said. "What's more impressive was that the studio let him go. He was under contract with one of the big Hollywood studios, and they weren't exactly thrilled to lose their leading man. By this time, he was already known as the King of Hollywood. But they let him go, and he went to officer training school, and then he was given the task of making a film to recruit aerial gunners to the army."

"Oh. So he joined the army but only made movies?" Janet finished arranging the pastries, and she checked to make sure the coffee was ready and the espresso machine was set.

"He was tasked with making a recruiting film, but he was the real deal. He flew several combat missions, and was even nearly killed when his plane was attacked. After that, studio executives lobbied to have him reassigned to safer tasks, and he was sent home to edit his film."

"I suppose they didn't want their big star killed."

"Of course they didn't. Back then, the Hollywood studios were very powerful. Gable apparently wanted another combat mission but was placed on inactive duty and eventually discharged from the army in June of 1944. He spent the next few months editing his recruiting film, *Combat America*, and finished his work on that in September 1944."

"And he showed up in Dennison later that month?"

"It seems so. He must have come to Dennison to work on the new film right after he finished the one the military had hired him to make."

"Does your book talk about what he was working on in Dennison?"

"There's just a couple of lines about it. It says his next project was supposed to be a film about the war effort at home, but when the footage he shot was stolen, he gave up the project and returned to Hollywood."

"So nothing we didn't already know."

"Not yet. That's as far as I made it last night, though. I'll keep reading and see if it says anything else."

"You must have been up pretty late, reading all that."

"I couldn't sleep. I was too ramped up from seeing that film. This is an unsolved mystery involving one of the biggest Hollywood stars in history. What if we were able to finally figure out what happened and how the film ended up in that theater?"

Debbie looked around the café, nodded, and walked over to the door, flipping the sign to Open.

"It would be pretty amazing," Janet said.

Patricia Franklin was their first customer of the day, stopping by to get her regular peppermint mocha, and she chatted with Janet and Debbie for a few minutes as her coffee brewed.

"I heard you all found something interesting yesterday," Patricia said, smiling as she handed over her credit card. Patricia was a local attorney and the granddaughter of their favorite octogenarian, Harry Franklin.

"We didn't find it ourselves," Janet called through the pass-through to the kitchen. She was prepping the grill for the morning rush.

"But yes, it's pretty cool," Debbie said. "How did you hear that already?"

"Small-town magic," Patricia said with a shrug. Then, as Janet handed her card back, she added, "Ellie from the library is in my book club. She told us."

"That makes more sense," Debbie said.

"You should ask my grandfather about it," Patricia said. "He used to talk about Clark Gable's visit to town sometimes. I think Pop Pop even met him while he was here, which he'd be happy to tell you all about, I'm sure."

"We'll be sure to ask him in that case." Patricia's grandfather Harry was in his late nineties and had been a porter at the depot during the war. He was also one of their regular customers and came in for breakfast most mornings.

"That will keep him out of trouble." Patricia lifted her coffee in a salute. "Have a great day."

"You too."

A rush of customers came in after that, and Janet and Debbie were kept busy making lattes and cooking eggs. Then just after nine, Harry Franklin came in, his dog Crosby trotting beside him. He took his regular seat at the counter, and Crosby sat at his feet.

"Good morning, Harry." Janet handed him the laminated menu, even though he knew it by heart by now. "How are you today?"

"The Lord woke me up this morning, so I can't complain." Harry laughed and asked for eggs and toast. He set the menu down on the counter.

"Hey, Harry, do you remember when Clark Gable visited Dennison?" Janet asked. "It was in 1944, I believe."

"Of course I remember when the King of Hollywood showed up in town," Harry said. "It was the dark days of the war—not that there were ever good days—and there was just bad news everywhere, and then, incredibly, the biggest movie star there was showed up in Dennison. Yes, I remember that. I was starstruck, along with everybody else in town."

"What do you remember about that time?" Janet asked.

Harry set his napkin in his lap. "He was making a movie. It was just a documentary about the war effort at home, but you would have thought appearing in this film was the kind of thing that would make you a movie star, the way everyone was trying to get in on it. People you normally saw wearing house dresses and slippers suddenly started parading around town in taffeta and pin curls. Of course, maybe some of those women were just trying to catch his eye, now that I think about it. I don't know. But the men were just as bad, hanging around wherever he was, trying to catch a glimpse of him. I just think we all needed a little distraction, and he sure provided one."

"Did you have any interactions with him?"

"I did speak with him once," Harry said. "When he came to the station to interview Eileen Turner. You could just tell he thought it was incredible that a woman had taken on the role of stationmaster while the men were away at war, so he spent a good long while interviewing her here at the depot."

Janet wanted to tell him that they'd seen the interview, but since she hadn't told him about the footage yet, she just nodded.

"He was at the station a couple of days, as I recall, but what I remember is that one day he filmed a train coming in and soldiers exiting the train. Well, I was helping the men off the train and directing them toward the canteen and the bathroom. They just stopped here for a short while, most of them, so I wasn't unloading trunks and that kind of thing. But afterward, Gable told me that he'd noticed how kind I was to the men." He fingered the paper placement in front of him on the counter, curling up the corner with his finger. "Said it was like I truly wanted to welcome them to Dennison. That comment stuck with me, and not just because it was a big star who said it. I remember it because that's exactly what I strove to do, to make the soldiers feel welcome, and it meant a lot that he had seen that."

"That's really special," Janet said. His pride in Gable's comment was evident, even all these years later. "I bet you always did a great job of that."

"I tried. But it was nice to be recognized for it. He didn't have to say that. He didn't even have to notice me. He was this big star, and I was just a porter at the railroad station."

"Not *just* a porter," Janet said. "That station couldn't have run without the work you did."

"Well, it was nice of him, anyway." Harry curled the paper place mat up and then pressed it back down.

Janet saw she had a line starting to form at the register, but it looked like Harry was about to say more, so she waited.

"Then, later that night, when I saw him at the theater, he recognized me and waved."

"We'd heard that he went to the theater while he was in town," Janet said. "You went too?"

"Everybody went to the theater back in those days," Harry said. "We didn't have televisions or streaming on our laptops. Movies were the entertainment. This was the golden age of Hollywood, and there were so many films coming out all the time. I was young and had no real responsibilities and a little pocket money, so I went as much as I could."

Janet had been wondering something and decided to ask Harry. "Did it strike you as odd that a film star would go to the movies too?" It seemed like celebrities these days went out of their way to stay out of the public eye when they weren't performing. "Was he just, like, sitting there with everyone else?"

"It didn't appear odd at the time. Don't writers read other people's books? Or musicians listen to music written by other people? Why wouldn't he watch films to see what was coming out and doing well?" He shrugged. "To answer your second question, people gave him space. I don't think anyone, even the boldest of the pin curl women, dared to take the seat right next to him. But like I said, everyone went to the movies back then. The theater was doing so well, Stanley Hersey had to install a second screen. That was rare in those days. Though I do think more people probably went while Clark was in town. When word got out that he spent his evenings taking in films, I suspect more than a few people started going to the theater hoping to catch a glimpse of him. That probably worked out just fine for Stanley Hersey."

"I'm sure he didn't mind it," Janet said.

"Course, then the film he was working on was stolen, and that was a sad day. He stuck around for a little while after that, but then when it didn't turn up, he left town, and I can't say I blame him. I don't think they ever did find it."

"They didn't," Janet said. "Until now."

"What?" Harry's head snapped up.

"Greg Connor found it in the old theater that's being renovated."

"Are you serious?"

Just then the bell in the kitchen dinged, and Janet knew she had to get back to work. "I am serious. Hold on. I'll tell you more in a minute. Let me get these orders taken care of."

Janet returned to the counter and rang up several customers, making lattes and serving pastries, and then retrieved Harry's plate from the window to the kitchen and set it in front of him.

"Are you sure Greg found the Clark Gable film?" Harry asked.

"I don't see what else it could be," Janet said. "He's in the footage interviewing people. It's definitely him."

"If that's true, that's a very big deal. Do you know how much that film could be worth?"

"I don't really know." Janet was interested in the film rolls for their historical value, not their monetary value.

"Clark Gable's stolen film? Lots of people would pay good money for that. I hope it's kept somewhere safe."

"It is." No need to mention it was a just few feet away in the café's safe.

"Good." Harry unrolled his silverware and picked up his fork. "Have you seen it?"

"I have. There's an old projector in the museum, and we were able to view it yesterday. Would you like to see it?"

"I would indeed."

Janet pulled out her phone and started playing the video she had taken. She set it down in front of Harry and went to go take more orders. When she finally returned to him, his plate was empty and he had tears in his eyes.

"It brings it all back, seeing it again," he said.

"It's pretty amazing, isn't it?"

"It is." Harry used his napkin to dab at his eyes. "Do you know how it ended up in the theater?"

"Not yet."

"But you're looking into it?"

"Not officially."

A slow smile spread across his face. "You'll figure it out."

Janet hoped so too. But for now, she had another question. "Do you have any idea who took it?"

"Oh, I wouldn't know," Harry said. "I was around then, but I wasn't involved in all that."

"But you must have heard some theories about it," Janet said.

Harry grinned at her over the rim of his ceramic coffee cup. "Rumors aren't worth much."

Janet leaned forward, waiting.

"The theory that was floated most often was that it was some-one from the hotel, since only someone at the hotel would have had access to his room," Harry said.

"It doesn't sound like you believe that."

"They tried to pin it on May Johnson. I knew May since the time I was in diapers. May didn't give a hoot about some Hollywood star and wouldn't have known what to do with that film if she had it."

"Wait. Who was May?"

"She was a maid at the hotel. She cleaned Gable's room. The police tried to say it was her who stole the film. But she was a true woman of faith. She taught Sunday school when I was a kid. She was as honest as they come. There is no way May had anything to do with taking that footage."

"Did the police investigate her?"

"Boy, did they. For a while we all thought they were going to get away with pinning it on her. We had prayer meetings about it. In the end, they had no evidence against her, because she didn't do it."

Janet processed this. The newspapers had said that a maid had been questioned, but it hadn't occurred to her that Harry might have known her.

"What was May's last name again?"

"Johnson. May Johnson. Her brother was the preacher of our church back then."

Janet scribbled the name on a napkin. "So who do you think did it, if not May?" she tried again.

"I don't know." He took another sip from his mug. "I'd say the studio producer who was hanging around, if I had to name someone."

"Why?"

"He was slimy. He just had this sense about him, and you could see it in the way he interacted with everyone. Like he thought he was better than everybody else."

"You saw the Hollywood producer?" A producer had been mentioned in the newspaper articles they'd read.

"Sure. He spent enough time in town, didn't he? Trying to get Clark to quit with the film and go back to make movies for him?"

"So he was in town before the theft?"

"Oh yes. Nearly as long as Gable himself. He wanted Clark to return to Hollywood, badly."

"Wait. So Clark wasn't making the film for the studio after all?"

"The rumor was Clark was making it on his own, and that's what had the studio all hot and bothered. He wasn't supposed to do his own work, not while he was under contract with them. That's what they said, anyway." Harry shrugged. "I never talked to him myself. But if the rumors were right, the producer's got the best reason to steal the film, doesn't he? If the film goes away, Gable gives up on the film he's not supposed to be making and comes back to Hollywood and stars in more movies for the studio. And that's exactly what happened, isn't it?"

Janet supposed it *was* what had happened.

"So there you go."

Janet didn't know if he was right, but that was a second vote for the studio executive. It was probably time to start finding out more about him.

But in the meantime, she had a line of customers. Time to get back to work.

CHAPTER SEVEN

Janet and Debbie were finished cleaning up and had already sent Paulette home. They had some time before they needed to leave for Steubenville to see Max Hersey, so Janet grabbed an order pad and a pen and said, "Okay, let's make a list."

"Anything in particular?" Debbie asked. "Or should I tell you what's on my shopping list?"

"A list of people to talk to," Janet said. "We're already going to talk to Max Hersey—"

"Hopefully the theater owner's son will be able to tell us something about how the film ended up in the theater wall."

"But failing that, I was thinking we should probably talk to Eileen." Janet wrote the name on the pad.

"Definitely. Since she was featured in the footage, we know she met Gable," Debbie said. "We could talk to Ray too." Both Eileen Palmer and Ray Zink lived at the Good Shepherd Retirement Center in town. "I don't think Ray was around while Clark was here, but his mom and his sister Gayle were in the footage. Maybe he could tell us about them."

"We should talk to Gayle too," Janet said.

"I think I have her number," Debbie said. "I can call her later."

"Perfect." Janet tapped her pen on the counter. "Who else?"

"It's not a long list, is it?"

"Not yet. What we need is more information about the suspects. Who the police talked to, what evidence there was, that kind of thing."

"We need the old police file," Debbie said.

"Do you think that still exists?" It seemed unlikely. "It's been eighty years. Do the police keep records for that long?"

"I don't know," Debbie said. "If it's a cold case, and a famous one at that, they might. But we have a little bit of time, right?

"We should have enough."

"There's only one way to find out."

A few minutes later, they locked up the café, packed some cookies to take to Max, and drove over to the police station in Janet's car. After walking up the stone steps and heading inside, Veronica, the receptionist, greeted them at the front of the office.

"Good afternoon, Janet, Debbie. How are you?" Her earrings swayed as she looked up at them.

"We're just fine," Janet said. "And you?"

"Doin' all right," Veronica said in a thick New York accent. Veronica had grown up in New York City and put up with no nonsense, which no doubt helped her manage this job. "I wrenched my back lifting a bag of potting soil the other day, but I've been icing it, and it's been better. That's what I get for trying to get a jump on my garden, I guess."

"I'm sorry to hear that," Debbie said. "Back injuries are the worst."

"It'll heal," Veronica said, shrugging. "Should I let Ian know you're here? He's in a meeting right now, but I can get him if you need me to." Behind Veronica, several officers typed on their computers or talked in low voices.

"That's okay. We're actually not here to see Ian," Janet said.

Veronica gave her a strange look. "In that case, what can I do for you?"

It was overly warm in the station office, and it smelled like sweat and stale coffee. Janet unzipped her jacket and took off her knit hat. "We were hoping it would be possible to get access to an old police file," she said.

"How old are we talking?" Veronica cocked her head.

"Really old," Debbie said. "From the 1940s."

Veronica let out a low whistle. "That's really old, all right."

"Do records from that time exist?" Janet asked.

"I don't know."

For a moment, Janet worried that the files might have been in the police storage area of the municipal warehouse that burned down the previous summer, but then Veronica continued.

"There are a bunch of old files in the basement, but I don't know if they go back that far. I can look around, I guess." She sounded dubious, like she was hoping they would say not to bother, but Janet nodded.

"That would be great. Isn't there a form we need to fill out?" Janet and Debbie had requested police files in the past.

"Here you go." Veronica opened a drawer and pulled a form out of a file folder. "Just fill this out with as much information as you have, and I'll see what I can find." She slid the paper across the counter.

"Thank you," Janet said. She took a pen from the cup on the counter and started filling out the form.

"It may take a day or two," Veronica said. "I'll have to poke around down there in between my regular duties."

"That's fine," Janet said. As anxious as she was to get her hands on the file, if it existed, she knew that Veronica already had plenty to do. Ian liked to joke that this station couldn't function without her, but Janet was pretty sure he truly meant it.

Janet filled in as much information as she could about the case file. *September 1944*, she put in the date line. *Clark Gable*, she wrote in the name line, and *theft* in the line to list the suspected crime.

She slid it back across the counter, and Veronica's eyes widened when she saw what she had written. "I should have known you guys would be looking into that one," she said. "The chief and some of the other officers were talking about it yesterday. If there's a file for this one, I bet they already pulled it."

"We'd love to see it, if so," Janet said.

"I'll ask the chief when he gets out of his meeting," she said. "Is there anything else I can help you with?"

"That's it for now," Debbie said. "Thank you."

"Any time."

They got back to the car, and Janet turned on the engine. Hot air blasted out of the vents.

"We've still got a little time," Debbie said. "Are you interested in making one more stop?"

"Where?"

"In Cadiz. It's right on the way, and if we're quick, we should still make it in time to meet Max."

"What's in Cadiz?" Janet asked.

"The house where Clark was born is now a museum," Debbie said. "I was thinking we might stop by and just check it out."

"Huh." Janet considered this. "You think the museum might be able to help us figure out who stole the film he was making?"

"Well, no, that doesn't seem especially likely," Debbie said. "But you never know. If nothing else, it might give us a better sense of who Clark Gable was and where he came from."

"Okay, why not?"

"All right." Debbie programmed the address into the map app on her phone, and soon they were on their way.

Traffic was light, and it only took a half hour to get to Cadiz. Shortly after they turned off the highway, they made it to the museum, where they drove past a sign that said CADIZ, BIRTHPLACE OF CLARK GABLE. A line drawing showed his face in silhouette.

"Looks like we're in the right spot," Janet said.

The museum was a two-story white house with a covered porch. They parked next to the building and made their way toward the door. They passed a stone tablet in front of the house that was engraved with Gable's face, and the words:

CLARK GABLE, KING OF HOLLYWOOD

WILLIAM CLARKE GABLE, STAGE AND MOTION PICTURE ACTOR, WAS BORN IN CADIZ, OHIO, ON FEBRUARY 1, 1901, IN A HOUSE THAT ONCE STOOD ON THIS SITE. HE WAS REARED IN NEARBY HOPEDALE. DURING HIS FILM CAREER OF 36 YEARS, GABLE MADE 67 TALKING PICTURES, INCLUDING IT HAPPENED ONE NIGHT, FOR WHICH HE WON AN OSCAR

IN 1934 AS BEST ACTOR AND THE CLASSIC GONE WITH THE WIND, WHICH WON THE ACADEMY AWARD FOR BEST PICTURE IN 1939. HE DIED NOVEMBER 16, 1960, IN HOLLYWOOD, CALIFORNIA.

"So it wasn't actually this house?" Janet asked. "Is that what this means?"

"Right," Debbie said. "The actual house he was born in was demolished in 1960. This is a replica."

Inside the museum, they found a large collection of memorabilia, including posters advertising the star's movies, still shots, pictures of Gable with various Hollywood starlets and several of his five wives, and plates, bowls, ashtrays, dish towels, and all kinds of items with his face on them.

They left the museum a half hour later with just enough time to get to Max's house. Debbie routed to the address in her GPS, and they pulled away from the museum.

"What did you think?" Debbie asked as soon as they were on the highway again.

"Well, I'm not sure I learned anything more about the real Clark Gable," Janet said. The museum was more a collection of memorabilia than any source of information explaining the star's life.

"I do have a fresh appreciation for how big of a star Clark Gable truly was in his day," Debbie said. "They put his face on everything."

"It is kind of amazing," Janet said.

Debbie adjusted one of the air vents to point toward her. "Having seen all that, I can see why it was such a big deal that he came to

Dennison to film his next movie. If any of the huge celebrities today did such a thing, it would be all over the news. Everyone around the world would know what they had for breakfast and could comment on it."

"True, although I don't know if every move celebrities made and everything they ate was reported on as fastidiously then as it is today," Janet said.

"They didn't have phones that could take videos of everything celebrities did," Debbie agreed. "And gossip websites and TV shows weren't really a thing, but newspapers and radio reported on what they did. The technology has changed, but I don't think the fascination with celebrities has."

"It sounds awful, doesn't it?" Janet said. "I can't imagine wanting to be famous, to have people watching your every move."

"I suppose to some people, it sounds pretty great," Debbie said. "To have millions of people know your name, and have your work admired."

"I do want my work to be respected," Janet said. "I hope that people enjoy what we do. But I can't say I've ever felt the need to have millions of people know my name. I'm more concerned with making the people I know and care about feel loved."

"I'm with you," Debbie said. "But what if you had the chance to have a cooking show? You wouldn't want that?"

"Not especially," Janet said.

Debbie thought for a moment, and then shook her head. "I don't think I would either. Too much pressure. Now, a cookbook, that would be a different story. Are you still thinking about making a cookbook?"

Janet turned her head. "I'm thinking about it." She fought to keep her voice level.

"I think it's a great idea," Debbie said. "You could use your own recipes, like we said before, but wouldn't it be cool if we also collected the recipes used at the Whistle Stop Café, both now and back in the day, and sold it at the restaurant? I bet we'd sell a ton of them."

"Now that's an interesting idea." Janet tried her best to keep her expression mild. She couldn't tell Debbie she was working on exactly such a project. She already had a stack of recipes from the World War II era they'd tried out at the café. There were the Navy's World War II soft sugar cookies. There was the eggless, milkless, butterless cake Betty Crocker had shown women how to make during wartime rations. She also planned to include the Salvation Army Doughnut Lassie recipe, which was the recipe for the doughnuts the volunteers would give out to service personnel coming through the station during the war. Janet still used the same recipe when they brought out the fryer for special occasions.

"I think it would be neat," Debbie said.

"I agree it's a great idea," Janet said. Her mind worked as she drove. She was glad she had proof that Debbie would enjoy the gift, but she would have to be extra careful that Debbie didn't discover she was already working on the cookbook. Would it take extra work to make it into something others might buy? And could she still get it ready in time to give to Debbie before her wedding?

Fifteen minutes later, they arrived at the entrance to the neighborhood where Max Hersey lived. There were big stone walls surrounding the beautifully landscaped green areas, lush with colorful flowers even as the temperatures hovered in the forties, and heavy metal gates blocked off the road. Fieldstone Estates was written in a script font on one of the walls. Janet slowed and stopped in front of the gates and entered the code Max had given her, and the gates swung open.

"Whoa," Debbie said as they passed by the first few houses in the development. The homes were huge, hulking things, designed in faux-Tudor and -Mediterranean styles. They were impressive, and Janet supposed that was the point. The houses on the south side of the road faced a golf course, a sprawling green lawn spreading out down a gentle slope toward a pond.

"You didn't tell me your dad's friend was loaded," Debbie said.

"I didn't know. He's certainly never come off that way. He's just a normal guy."

"A normal guy with an exclusive country club membership and an astronomical HOA fee, no doubt," Debbie said as they passed the clubhouse for the golf course. Several golf carts were parked in the lot in front of the clubhouse, along with half a dozen cars with high-end brand names.

"Max's house should be just up ahead," Janet said as she turned onto a side street. They passed expansive, beautifully landscaped yards and finally pulled up in front of a brick neoclassical-style house with fluted columns holding up a hip roof with dormers.

"I don't know. It doesn't have a very good view of the golf course," Debbie said. "I hope they got a discount for that."

Janet shook her head. "Come on." She grabbed the plate of cookies they had packed for Max and walked up the long fieldstone walkway to the oversized front door. They rang the doorbell, and it echoed. A dog started barking from somewhere inside the house, and the noise got closer until the door opened.

"Janet." Max smiled and opened his arms to give her a hug. Max was tall, solid, and wore a sweater vest over a button-down and khakis. A fluffy little white dog yapped at his feet.

"Hi, Max. You remember my friend Debbie?" Janet stepped inside and gave Max a hug, and he wrapped his arms around her.

"Of course." He pulled back and then gave Debbie a hug. "It's great to see you again. Thank you for coming." He ushered them in, closing the door behind him. "Just ignore Bingo." The little dog continued to bark. "He thinks he's a scary guard dog."

The entryway had a soaring, double-height ceiling over a wide staircase that turned halfway up. To the left was what looked like a formal sitting room, to the right was a dining room with a long table, and up ahead was a large open space.

"This is beautiful," Janet said, walking through the room to a cluster of couches gathered around a wall of windows that looked out over the backyard.

"Thank you," Max said. "It's all a bit much if you ask me, but Ling fell in love, so here we are."

"How is Ling?" Janet remembered meeting Max's wife a few times, though she often traveled for work as an executive at some big company and didn't seem to be around much.

"She's doing well. She's in Singapore at the moment, but she comes back Saturday, and then we head out to Italy for our anniversary. Bingo and I miss her when she's gone, but I'm glad she gets to do something she loves. I keep trying to get her to retire or at least slow down, but I don't know if she ever will."

They followed him toward the rear of the house. He gestured to the couch on one side of a low coffee table while he sat on the other.

Behind him was a kitchen with light wood cabinets and a huge island topped with marble and what looked like a professional-grade stove. "How is Ian?"

They chatted for a while about Janet's life and family, and he told them about his children and grandchildren. Then he leaned forward and said, "So, what's this about film turning up at the old theater?"

Janet and Debbie explained that the old building had been bought by someone who wanted to turn it back into a working theater and had started renovating.

"That's wonderful news," Max said. "My dad would have been so happy to hear that it was going to show movies again."

"Your parents ran the theater for a long time," Debbie said.

"They opened it in 1939," he said. "It seems crazy that it was so long ago. They were young and saw an opportunity, and my dad had always loved films, so they went for it. They got a loan, and found all the equipment needed, and turned an empty space in town into the cinema. The studios were pumping out film after film, and there was an insatiable desire for more. The public just couldn't get enough."

"So the theater was a success," Debbie said.

"It did well enough," he said. "Of course, Mom and Dad ran things mostly by themselves, and for a while things were great. It was the only theater in the area, and it had two screens, which Dad was especially proud of. When I came along in 1953, were spending so much time at the theater I basically grew up there. It's not a bad place to hang out when you're a kid. It certainly made it easy to make friends. Who wouldn't want to be friends with the boy who can get you free movies and popcorn?"

"I'm sure that's not why people were friends with you," Janet said.

Max laughed. "Well, not the ones who mattered. Your father and I just clicked from the moment we started playing soldier together on the playground."

"So you weren't born yet when Clark Gable visited Dennison," Debbie said.

"No, but my dad talked about it for the rest of his life," Max said. "He had shown so many of Gable's films at the theater, and then here he was, in person, right here in Dennison."

"We heard that Gable came to the theater several times while he was in town," Janet said.

"That's right. Most nights, from what I understand. Of course, listening to my dad, you would have thought he and Clark Gable had become best buddies, though I can't imagine that's true. But it was something he talked about, for sure, even in his later days. It was one of the highlights of his career, I think."

"Did he ever talk about the film that Gable was working on that got stolen?"

"Of course. It was still heartbreaking for him, even years later. Dad was interviewed for the film, I guess, and he always thought having the theater featured in the film would be great for business. Plus, I think, like anyone, he was looking forward to seeing Gable's latest production, and it was a bonus that it was going to feature so many people and places from Dennison."

"Did your dad have any idea what happened to the film?" Debbie asked.

"Not as far as I know," Max said. "Like I said, it was something he talked about sometimes, how disappointed he was that the film never got made. I think he always felt like Clark gave up too easily and should have started over instead of abandoning the project altogether. I'm confident he had no idea those film canisters ended up inside the theater. Dad wouldn't have let them stay hidden for all that time if he'd known, I know that for sure." He smiled. "He would have lost his mind to find out where it had been this whole time. Where in the theater was it?"

"Stuck inside a wall at the rear of one of the auditoriums," Janet said. "Behind the concession stand but on the auditorium side."

"Wow." He shook his head.

"Do you have any ideas about how the film could have ended up there? You knew that theater better than anyone. Was there any kind of opening in that wall that could have allowed for it to be slipped in? An electrical panel, or anything like that?"

"Not that I know of. That was just a wall, I'm nearly positive. I would have to get ahold of old plans to know for sure, but I don't think so."

"Greg—that's the contractor—" Debbie started.

"And Debbie's fiancé," Janet added.

"Congratulations," Max said.

"Thank you." Debbie smiled. "Anyway, Greg thinks it must have been put there during the renovation, when the theater changed to two screens."

"That seems plausible," Max said. "But who would do that?"

Janet looked over at Debbie, who was watching Max closely. Max was quiet for a moment before he nodded. "Right. I see what you're getting at. You think maybe Dad put it there. Buried it behind the wall at some point."

"Or your mom, or someone else who worked at the theater at the time," Janet said.

"Or someone involved in the renovation project," Debbie added.

"It does seem the most likely scenario that someone who knew the theater intimately and had access to its ins and outs would be the one who hid the film," Janet added gently.

"The thing is, Dad would never have done that," Max said. His voice was—not emphatic, exactly, but certain. "I'm telling you, he always talked about how disappointed he was that Gable's movie set in Dennison never saw the light of day. Mom too. She thought he was such a great actor. Neither of them could have—"

Janet listened as he continued, not sure what to say. She had no way of knowing if Max's parents were involved with the missing footage. Max was sure they weren't, but kids didn't always know everything about their parents, especially in this case, since it all happened before Max was born. But the film being found in the theater did point to at least the possibility somebody knew more than they had said.

CHAPTER EIGHT

"I was doing some reading last night," Debbie said when she came into the café Wednesday morning. She held a bag of copies of the current issue of the *Gazette,* the weekly newspaper that they sold at the register along with vintage candies and gums and other nostalgic treats. The papers must have been delivered outside while Janet was baking.

"More of the Clark Gable biography?" Janet might have felt bad that she hadn't spent the evening researching as well, but she'd actually spent it trying to figure out how someone went about getting a cookbook made. She was pretty sure she wasn't going to interest a traditional publisher in producing the book, and there were plenty of services that allowed anyone to make, print, and sell their own books, but she didn't know how to tell one from another. She'd spent hours online, looking at various options, before getting frustrated and giving up. But she couldn't exactly tell Debbie any of that.

"Yes, partly." Debbie dropped the stack of newspapers on the counter, and then she set her purse down and peeled off her coat. "I got to the part where he returned to Hollywood after the war and started making films again. And got married again."

"Which number was this one?"

"Number four. Sylvia Ashley. She was a British model and actress."

"Did this one last?"

"I haven't gotten there yet, but, well, judging by the fact that we know there was a fifth Mrs. Gable, I'm going to guess probably not."

"That's too bad."

"Yeah, I started to get kind of depressed, so I did some googling to learn more about his life with his wives, and I found some old magazines that were pretty entertaining," Debbie said. "Gable had such a colorful personal life that he showed up regularly. I even found some recipes that were shared by his wives."

"Recipes from multiple wives?" Janet asked.

"Oh, sure. This magazine *Modern Screen* liked to profile the stars and talk about how they entertained. Gable's second wife Ria shared a pancake recipe that he liked. Then I found an article where his third wife Carole shared some summer recipes, including a salmon salad and a sparkling pineapple punch recipe. It was all so very 1940s. Maybe we should recreate some of the recipes here?"

"It might not be a bad idea. Though I don't really think it's summer salad weather." Even if they didn't add the recipes to the menu, maybe she could add them to the recipe book she was making. That could be fun. "Can I see them?"

"Sure. I'll email them to you." Debbie smiled. "After that, I started doing some research on Frederick Hallman."

"Who?"

"The studio executive who came to Dennison to convince Gable to ditch the home-front project and come back to Hollywood and start making real films."

"Oh, that guy. I'd forgotten his name. What did you learn about him?"

"Well, when I searched for him, the first thing that came up was his filmography."

"What did you find?"

"Frederick Hallman was involved in dozens of movies in the thirties and forties. He did various jobs, judging by his job titles, until he worked his way up to producer, and he helped produce many of Clark Gable's hit movies."

"Before the war, or after?"

"Both, it seems." Debbie slipped an apron over her head.

"Which means that he was successful in getting Gable back to Hollywood after the war."

"Which means he was successful in getting Gable back to Hollywood after his time in Dennison," Debbie clarified. "The question is, did he have any role in getting rid of the film footage to hasten that event along? That is what I don't know." Debbie walked over to the counter and untied the plastic bag around the newspapers. "I did find that he wrote a book in his later years, so I ordered a copy of it last night. It's long out of print, but I found a used copy online and paid for rush shipping. It should be here in a few days."

"Do you think he'll admit in the book that he stole Clark Gable's independent film to get him to Hollywood to start making money for the studio again?"

"I mean, it would be great if he did," Debbie said. "But I kind of doubt that would make it into print. We'll see what turns up. I'll keep you posted when it arrives."

"That sounds great."

Debbie slid the stack of newspapers from the bag and started to set them next to the register, but stopped.

"Have you seen this?" She held up a newspaper.

KING OF HOLLYWOOD'S STOLEN MOVIE DISCOVERED IN HISTORIC THEATER, the headline read. The article featured a picture of Sam Watson holding the film canisters in front of the theater, its art deco marquee still dilapidated and covered in paint. It was no doubt taken in the window between finding them in the theater and leaving them here at the café.

"Does it say anything we don't already know?" Janet asked.

"Hang on." Debbie skimmed the article, flipping from the first page to the third to finish reading the story. "Nope. Just the facts that we already know. Sam is doing renovations, found the film, played it on the projector at the Depot Museum, and discovered it was the missing Clark Gable film. Then there's some background on Gable's visit to town in 1944 and how the film was stolen, but there's not much more than that."

"That's too bad. I was hoping Jim might have unearthed something we haven't found yet."

"Apparently not." Debbie closed the newspaper and set it back on the stack. "Still, it's pretty cool to see it in print."

"It is," Janet agreed. "Anyway, what do you think about going to visit Eileen and Ray today after we close?"

"You read my mind. By the way"—Debbie fanned the papers out artistically on the counter—"the number I had for Gayle Zink doesn't work anymore. It's out of service."

"Maybe Ray can give us her new number," Janet said.

"That sounds like a good plan to me."

The found film was a hot topic in the café that afternoon. It seemed to be all anyone was talking about. Brenda Winston, Pastor

Nick's wife, had fond memories of seeing movies in the old theater when she was a teenager and couldn't believe the film had been there this whole time. Patricia Franklin wondered who might claim ownership and how a judge would rule about it. Debbie's father, Vance, showed up for lunch with several members of his men's group, and each of them had a theory about how the film ended up in the theater, each more outlandish than the next.

After they closed and cleaned up, Janet packed several boxes of cookies, and they climbed into Debbie's car and headed for Good Shepherd. The building sat on a rolling piece of land crisscrossed by walking paths and shaded by mature pine trees. There weren't any residents outside on this cold March day, but a few ducks swam along the surface of the pond. Inside, the home was warm and cozy, and Janet smiled at Ashley Cramer, the receptionist. They signed in and then went to find Eileen.

Debbie's father had managed the home until his retirement a couple years ago, so Debbie felt very comfortable here and knew most of the nurses.

"Who are you looking for?" asked Sonya, a nurse who had gone to high school with Janet and Debbie.

"Eileen and Ray," Debbie said.

"I don't know where Ray is, but I just saw Eileen in the sunroom, so you might try there," Sonya said.

"We will. Thank you."

They followed the long hallways and wound their way to the back of the building, where they found Eileen reading in a patch of sunlight. Ferns, African violets, and succulents hung from hooks and sat on tables all around the room. Outside, a stiff wind blew, shaking the branches on the surrounding pine trees, but this room was bright and warm. A grin broke across Eileen's face when she saw them.

"Hello there," she said. "It's good to see you both." Eileen had curly gray hair and big glasses, and though she was over one hundred, her mind was still sharp. Today she wore a wool sweater and had a fuzzy blanket over her lap. She placed a bookmark in her novel and set it on a side table next to her wheelchair.

"Hi, Eileen," Debbie said, leaning in to give her a hug. Once she'd pulled back, Janet leaned in for one as well. "How are you?"

"I can't complain," Eileen said. "Last night they served my favorite chocolate brownies, and now I have visitors, so life isn't too bad."

"I guess it's not," Janet said, chuckling. She sat in a padded chair across from Eileen, and Debbie sat next to her. "It's good to see you."

"It's great to see you both. Hey, did you read the newspaper this morning?" Eileen said. "Quite the scuttlebutt with finding that film. Kim tells me she was able to use an old projector she had at the museum to watch it. Can you imagine?"

"That's actually what we came here to talk to you about," Debbie said. "We were able to watch the film when Kim got the projector working, and you'll never guess who we saw featured in it."

Eileen laughed. "Kim told me. Well, I mean, of course I remember being interviewed. You never forget something like being interviewed by Hollywood's leading man—and a war hero to boot."

"Can you tell us about it?" Janet asked. "What do you remember about that time?"

"Oh, it was big news. It was all anyone talked about," Eileen said. "It was funny, because I don't think anyone knew he was coming to town before he showed up, camera in tow."

"I imagine that caused quite a stir," Janet said.

Eileen laughed. "I remember when my friend Edna told me she'd seen him down at the diner. I thought she was mistaken, of course, but she was insistent. I told her she'd lost her mind. Clark Gable had not come to our tiny little town and ordered a roast beef sandwich. But it turned out she was right, of course. People reported seeing him driving around town in a roadster and eating at the diner and attending the theater in the evenings. Boy, did that diner become a popular place overnight. The theater too. I don't know how many tickets they sold, with everyone hoping to catch a glimpse of him. You have to understand, back in his day, he was the biggest star around, so for him to show up here—well, it was quite the thing."

"When did you find out why he was in town?" Debbie asked.

"He just showed up at the station one day and asked for the stationmaster," Eileen said. "He didn't seem surprised that it was me, like most men were in those days. I was grateful for that, though I was totally starstruck. I couldn't believe it was really him, but it was."

"He came to ask you to be in his film?" Janet said.

"That's right. He said he was working on a movie about the war effort at home, and he had heard about the Dennison station and how we greeted the soldiers that came through, so he wanted to talk to me about it, and asked if I would be in his film."

"Did you have to think about it?"

"Not at all," Eileen said. "I thought that if the film could bring attention to the hard work the people in this town were putting in, it might help raise some funds for buying supplies for the meals we handed out, and it would be worth it. I said yes."

"And did he interview you that day? How did it work?"

"Oh, no," Eileen said. "I told him I would be happy to talk to him, but I couldn't do it until the next day. If I'm honest, I might have suggested that it was because of the train schedule that I couldn't squeeze him in, but the truth was my hair was a mess, and I hadn't brought lipstick or anything of the sort. I didn't bother with stuff like that most days—I had a job to do, and no one I was trying to impress—but if I was going to be in a movie, I was going to sleep with pin curls and put on some rouge."

"He was okay with that?"

"Seemed to be," Eileen said. "He returned the next day with his camera and set it up in the station waiting area, and then he turned on the camera and started asking questions."

"He did all this by himself?" Janet asked. "There wasn't anyone with him working on, say, lighting or sound?"

"Or setting up the camera? Weren't cameras enormous in those days?" Debbie added.

Eileen laughed. "As opposed to the phone everyone has in their pockets now, yes. But they weren't so big that one person couldn't handle it. It was basically a big box on a tripod, with two big film reels on top. They looked like Mickey Mouse ears, I always thought."

Janet thought she could picture it in her head. She'd have to look it up later, but she thought she knew what Eileen was talking about.

"What was it like, being interviewed by him?" Debbie asked.

"Oh, I was a nervous wreck, but he did his best to make me feel at ease. He asked about what we did here at the station, and we talked about why so many trains stopped here."

"Halfway between Columbus and Pittsburgh," Debbie said with a laugh.

"What is it they always say about real estate? Location, location, location?" Eileen smiled. "It would be so fun to see that footage again. Maybe I could convince Kim to lug that projector over here to show me."

"She doesn't need to do that," Janet said. She dug out her phone. "I recorded it as it played. Would you like to see?"

"Well, aren't you clever?" Eileen grinned. "Yes, I'd very much like to."

Janet pulled up the video and pressed play, and Eileen showed up on the screen.

"Oh my." Eileen pressed her lips together for a moment. Then she said, "I was a baby."

"You were in charge of the entire station," Debbie said with a touch of admiration.

They watched, as, on screen, Eileen explained how many trains went through Dennison Station each day and how the volunteers served free food to the service personnel who came through. By the time the segment featuring Eileen was over, she was shaking her head. "It's so strange to see it all again," she said. "It feels like it was just yesterday sometimes."

Janet pressed pause.

"I can't believe you found it, after all this time," Eileen said. "It was the biggest news when that film went missing. The police interviewed everybody in town, it seemed like, and no one knew anything. I think they even brought in the state police, if I'm remembering correctly. Everyone was trying to figure out what happened to that film."

"Who did you think had done it, back in the day?" Janet asked.

"Oh, I don't know." Eileen adjusted the blanket in her lap.

Janet looked at Debbie. Was she just being nice? Not wanting to cast aspersions on people? The way she said it, Janet thought she had some ideas.

"Surely you had a theory," Debbie said.

"Everyone in town had a theory," Eileen said. "Maybe none of them were right. I suppose now that we know where the film ended up, we'd have to look at things differently."

"Do you think it was someone at the theater?" Debbie asked.

"I truly couldn't say," Eileen said. "But what I couldn't figure out was, how would anyone have been able to get the film out of the room without the help of someone at the hotel?"

"Ah. So you think it was the maid?"

"May? Oh, no. They tried to pin it on her, sure, but she was the sweetest thing. She would never have done something like that. Besides, she wasn't the only one who would have had access to the key to that room. I guess I always assumed the hotel manager, Bernard, might have had something to do with it. After all, the whole place had heard him threaten to throw Clark out if he didn't pay up. The police thought it might be him too. But I don't know. They never did manage to find proof, I guess. Maybe he didn't have anything to do with it after all. Who knows?" She let out a little sigh.

The room was quiet for a moment. From somewhere down the hall, Janet heard two women talking about whether the chef did noodles or beef better in the dining room. Janet tried to figure out whether she could get Eileen to say more about the hotel manager.

"Could I see the rest of the film?" Eileen gestured at the phone again.

"Of course," Janet said. She backed the footage up and started it playing from the end of Eileen's interview, and then the scene shifted to the canteen, where Gayle Bailey—Gayle Zink then—smiled and stood next to the woman who explained what the volunteers were doing in the café.

"Gayle!" Eileen clapped her hands. "She was so young. She was such a firecracker."

"Still is," Debbie said.

"Naturally." Eileen's lips curled up in a smile. "And Dolores Zink. That's her mom. Now she was a kind woman."

"Did you know her?" Janet asked.

"Not well. But every time I interacted with her, she was lovely."

On the screen, footage played of the interview with Stanley Hersey at the old theater.

"This is where the first film reel ended, and we had to load up the second one," Janet explained as the video stopped. "But hang on. I have another video of the second reel." She swiped to the right, and the next video came up.

On screen, trains came into the station, and Clark conducted more interviews inside the canteen. There were the conversations with the soldiers, including Danny Maldanado, who were coming through the station. Several of the boys—young men, she probably was supposed to call them, but they truly were little more than boys—looked as starstruck as the women in the canteen had been. There were also the other interviews Clark had conducted with the minister and the ladies' auxiliary, and then the interview with the hotel manager came on.

"There he is," Eileen said. "Bernard Williams."

"The manager at the hotel," Janet said as she pressed pause.

"He doesn't look especially upset at Clark," Debbie said.

"This must have been early in his stay," Eileen said. "Before he'd gone two weeks without paying."

"We read about that in the paper," Debbie said. "What was the story there?"

"Oh, I don't know. Something about how Clark hadn't paid for his stay. I didn't hear the altercation firsthand and can only tell you rumor, which isn't worth much."

Janet pressed play again, and the scene shifted once again, and the shot of the inside of the Delancey Diner showed up.

"Helen?!" Eileen exclaimed.

"Wait. What?" Janet paused the video. On the screen, Clark sat next to the teenager in the diner's uniform. "You know who that is?"

"It's Helen Fletcher," Eileen said, but she shook her head, like she wasn't sure. "She would have been McDonald then, I suppose, but it's her."

"Who was she?"

"Helen was my friend Lenore's sister. You would know her as Doreen Fletcher's mother. Colleen Kelly's grandmother. I'd forgotten she was a waitress there. But what is she doing sitting there with Clark Gable?"

Janet tried to wrap her mind around this. That made Helen the great-great-grandmother of Ashling Kelly, one of Tiffany's good friends.

"Let me see what happens," Eileen said. Janet started the video again, and they watched as teenaged Helen told Clark Gable they might star together in a movie someday.

"She's got confidence, you have to give her that," Eileen said when the scene shifted and Janet had paused the film again.

"I take it she never made it to Hollywood?" Debbie asked.

"No, she didn't. She got married and settled down in her hometown and, by all accounts, had a beautiful life."

"I imagine she must have always treasured the memory of this meeting," Debbie said. But something in the way she said it made Janet think that wasn't what she was really saying.

"I suppose," Eileen said. "But what's strange is that I never knew about it. Back then, everyone was talking about Clark Gable, and anyone who caught a glimpse of him told it all over town. But if Lenore knew her sister had met him and had this conversation with him, I never heard about it."

"I suppose there are all kinds of reasons not to spread something like this around," Debbie said. "It was just a conversation in a diner. It never went anywhere. The film was never made, and she never became an actress." Again, though, the way Eileen said it, Janet knew she was asking a question that she wasn't saying aloud.

"Who knows why people do what they do," Eileen said. "I'm sure Helen had her reasons. Or maybe Lenore did know, and she chose not to spread it around. Helen always did get so much attention, because she was so pretty and had this big personality. Maybe Lenore didn't want Helen to get more attention. I don't know."

"Maybe."

No one spoke for a moment, and then Eileen said, "I will say, he was a terrible flirt. He even tried it with me, if you can believe it, but I wasn't about to fall for his lines. That smoldering smile was hard to resist, but he was so…Hollywood. I don't know. I knew it wasn't personal. I was a young woman, and I was there. It wasn't about me personally."

"You were able to resist the charm of the King of Hollywood?" Janet said.

"I was in love with Sam anyway. A Hollywood star held little charm for me. What I wanted at the time was an Amish farmer." Eileen reached out her hand so it touched a beam of sunlight pouring in through the window. "Thankfully, I eventually met Rafe and ended up with the right man. But no, I wasn't the kind of girl who was about to lose my mind because some celebrity glanced my way."

"Okay. So, Helen obviously knew this footage existed," Janet said.

"She can't have missed the camera in front of them."

"If, for whatever reason, she didn't want this footage to come out…" Janet started.

"But why wouldn't she? If she wanted to be an actress, what better exposure could there be?" Debbie asked.

"What about that line about the money?" Eileen said. "Where she said there were other ways to get money than saving tips."

"Oh." Janet saw that Eileen was right. What had Helen said? She backed up the footage and played that part again.

"Like I said, I've been making plans," Helen said on screen. "And I've been putting aside money."

"The tips here must be pretty good if you've been able to save up for a train ticket."

"I didn't say it all came from working here. There are other ways, you know. Though, I will say the tips have gotten bigger since I've been waiting on you."

"I just can't help myself around a pretty woman."

"Where was she getting money from, if not from tips?" Debbie asked when Janet paused the video again.

"And did she realize she'd get found out, if this footage was released?" Janet said. "Maybe she spoke out of turn and realized afterward she'd made a big mistake?"

Debbie nodded, thinking it through. "It sounds like she was stealing from someone. Or something. That's not the kind of thing you want revealed in a documentary."

"But is that enough of a reason for her to want the footage to be gone?" Janet asked.

"I don't know," Debbie said. "I suppose it depends on who she was stealing from and how much she'd stolen. It's possible Helen Fletcher might have wanted very badly to make sure no one ever saw it."

Debbie and Janet looked at each other, then at Eileen, who was also nodding.

They had a new suspect.

CHAPTER NINE

*A*fter Janet and Debbie had chatted with Eileen for a while, Eileen was ready to go to her room for a nap, so Debbie walked her back and called for a nurse and then set out to find Ray Zink. They found Ray at a table in the sitting room, working on a jigsaw puzzle of puppies wearing red bows. Half a dozen residents were positioned in front of the television, watching some daytime talk show, but Ray didn't seem to be paying attention to the screen at all.

"Good afternoon, Ray," Janet called, and he looked up, a smile breaking across his face.

"Well, hello there. Fancy meeting you here."

"Do you have a minute to talk?" Debbie asked.

"Well, let me think. I have a lot going here, as you can see, but I might be able to fit you in." He wheeled back from the table. "Maybe we should go to my room, where we won't disturb everyone?"

"That sounds great." Debbie stepped forward and grasped the handles of Ray's wheelchair, steering him expertly through the hallways to his room. She parked his wheelchair next to the small sitting area in his room, and she and Janet sat down in the two chairs by the window.

"So what brings the two of you by today?" Ray asked.

"We were hoping you might be able to help us get in touch with Gayle," Janet said. "We tried calling her, but the number we have doesn't seem to be in service any longer."

"Oh, I see how it is." Ray laughed. "It's my sister you really want to talk to. Well, I'll take visitors, no matter why they end up coming to me."

"We're delighted to see you," Janet said, but Ray shook his head.

"I'm only kidding. Of course I can put you in touch with Gayle. Her granddaughter got her a new phone for Christmas. One of those fancy doodads that can do your laundry and everything else."

"She got a new number too?" Usually you kept your number when you got a new phone these days.

"She kept getting too many spam calls on her old number. I don't know that a new number is going to change anything, but what do I know? Hold on. Let me see. I have the new number written down here somewhere."

Ray wheeled himself over to the small desk area and opened a leather-bound address book. He flipped through the pages and ran his finger down one. "Okay. Ready?"

He read out the number, and both Janet and Debbie entered it into their smartphones—their doodads—and saved it.

"Can I ask what is it you want to talk to Gayle about?" Ray asked, closing the address book.

"Of course," Debbie said. "It's about Clark Gable."

"Oh, she'll be happy to talk about him, that's for sure," he said. "Did you know he came to Dennison once?"

"We did," Janet said.

"She saw him a bunch of times while he was in town. He even smiled at her once, at the local theater, and I'm sure she'll tell you all about it."

"That's actually what we wanted to talk to her about," Janet said. "It seems that while he was here, he was making a movie, and we were recently able to see it."

"You were?" He blinked. "The stolen film reels. You found them?"

Evidently Ray hadn't seen the newspaper today.

"Well, we didn't find them, personally," Debbie said. "But we were able to view them, and sure enough, Gayle is on one of them, along with someone we assume must be her mother. Your mother. They were at the canteen."

"Really?" He chuckled. "Mother did volunteer there, didn't she?" And then, a moment later, he said, "Where were the film rolls?"

"At the old theater," Janet said. "They turned up because they're doing renovations to turn it back into a theater. They were behind a wall."

"Huh." Ray rubbed his temple, processing this news. "Well, isn't that something? I guess no one thought to look there."

"No, I don't think anyone did," Janet said. "We're trying to figure out how it got there. Since we knew Gayle was in the footage, we thought we'd talk to her."

"I'm sure Gayle would be thrilled to tell you about it," Ray said. "She was so sorry that the movie was never made. Seeing Clark Gable, well, that was very exciting for her. She even wrote to me over in Holland to tell me about it. She was young, of course, and with the war on, there wasn't a lot for young girls to get excited about, I guess. I think she was a little starstruck."

"I get the sense many people were," Debbie said.

"Of course, now that we know that the theater was where the film went after it was stolen, we're particularly interested in finding out more about anyone who was there," Janet said. "You said that's where Gayle saw him?"

"That's what she said in her letter to me, if I'm remembering it right." He nodded. "I wasn't around then, so I don't know for sure."

"Did Gayle tell you anything about the theater back then? Or did she see anything?"

"You'd have to ask her," he said. "I'm afraid I don't know."

"That's quite all right," Debbie said. "You were off fighting in the war. I can't imagine the comings and goings of a celebrity were of great interest to you."

"A celebrity who was also a veteran, don't forget," Ray said. "He may have been a Hollywood star, but he also flew combat missions, which meant he was one of us."

Janet smiled to hear the pride in Ray's voice.

"He was indeed," Debbie said.

There was a beat of silence, and then Ray said, "You know, Mother always followed Clark's career, which was odd because she didn't care one whit about celebrities. Didn't approve of movies, honestly. But she always followed Gable because she knew his mother."

"Wait." Had Janet heard that right? "What?"

"Oh wow." Debbie seemed as surprised by the news as Janet was. Though, she realized it wasn't all that shocking. Clark Gable had been born nearby. This wasn't a huge metropolis. Gable's parents must have known people in the area. Still, what were the chances

Ray's mother would have been one of them? "What did your mother tell you about Addie?"

"Not a lot. Mother grew up in Cadiz and still lived there when Addie and Will Gable moved to town. Mother was hired to clean for them once a week. She was young then, barely a teenager, I think, but back then everyone did what they could to get by."

"Gable's family must have had some money, if they were hiring someone to clean," Janet said.

"I don't know," Ray said. "This was well before my time, obviously, so I can't say for sure. But when Mother talked about it, I got the sense that they needed help because the mother was sick in some way."

"The book I read said she might have had epilepsy or some other central nervous system problem," Debbie said.

Ray scratched his chin. "Maybe that was it."

"You don't think that was it," Janet said.

"I wouldn't know. But that's why Mother always followed his career, because she'd met him when he was a baby."

"Did she say anything more about him?"

"Not a lot. Or if she did, I didn't listen." He shrugged. "She might have said more, but I was a young man and had other interests than gossip about people my mother knew."

"Understandable," Debbie said.

"I wish I had paid more attention," Ray said. "Gayle may be able to tell you more."

"We'll ask her," Janet said. "Now, if you can't tell us anything more about Clark Gable's visit to town, tell us how you are doing."

Ray chatted with them about a recent bingo night at the center, and about a visit from his niece, and shared a funny story about a woman down the hall who had a habit of breaking into show tunes whenever someone asked her a question she didn't want to answer. A half hour later, they walked out into the parking lot.

"That was a fascinating afternoon," Debbie said as they stepped outside. The bitter chill snaked up under Janet's coat, and she pulled it tighter around herself.

"It usually is, when you take the time to listen to an older person talk," Janet said. "They always have the best stories."

"That is true," Debbie agreed. "And it sounds like we have a new lead in addition to Gayle's phone number."

"It does sound like we need to see what we can find out about Helen Fletcher," Janet said.

"Maybe the best place to start there is to get in touch with Colleen Kelly," Debbie said. "As well as Gayle Bailey."

Janet nodded. "It sounds like it's time to divide and conquer."

They agreed that Janet would call Colleen. "I'm sure you can find a nice way to ask if she knows if her grandmother stole any money and then stole rolls of film to cover it up during the war," Debbie said.

Janet snorted. "I probably won't lead with that."

"So if you'll make those calls, I'll call Gayle," Debbie said. "We'll have this case cracked in no time."

CHAPTER TEN

When Janet got home, she called Colleen Kelly. Colleen had grown up here in town, but she was a few years older than Janet, so they hadn't really become friendly until Tiffany and Ashling had been in several activities together. When the girls were younger, Janet and Colleen's communications had mainly involved logistics of playdates and school pick-ups, but as they had gotten older, they had settled into an easy friendship.

Colleen's phone rang and rang, and then went to voice mail.

Janet left a message, asking Colleen to give her a call when she got a chance. She hung up and turned to the collection of recipes in front of her. She had managed to find the historic recipes at the café today, and with the Clark Gable recipes Debbie had sent her, she now had a pretty good collection of recipes she wanted to include. If she was going to be make a cookbook that other people would want to buy, she would need to make sure it was put together well and designed and published professionally.

One of the companies she had researched yesterday promised to do just that, so she spent some time poking around their website, and even typed in the recipe for the Navy's Sugar Cookies and worked on setting it up on the page. That looked pretty good, actually. There was a space where she could add a photo, if she wanted to, but Janet didn't think she would be able to get photographs of all the recipes. She decided this would just be a book of recipes, no photos. It seemed like that would keep the cost down too, which was helpful. This could work.

Ian came home while she was finishing up the asparagus and cheese tart she was making for dinner. Even though spring felt aspirational at this point in March, asparagus made it feel like it was almost here. She slid the tart into the oven and smiled when Ian walked into the house.

"Hey," Janet said. "How was your day?"

"Busy." He pulled off his coat. "But not with the drug case that we need to be spending our time on. We spent most of the day trying to figure out how to respond to the press that kept calling the station."

"What?" Janet set down the hot pads.

"We should have known the news story about that film would spread quickly. Look at this. It's on the front page of the *New York Times*." Ian held up his phone, and Janet walked over and squinted at the screen.

Missing Clark Gable Film Discovered in Small Town Ohio Theater, the headline read.

"Oh my goodness."

"It's everywhere, though. The AP, the BBC, all the national papers. Plus the TV networks have been calling too."

"Why would they call you?"

"They called Sam too. The poor guy—his phone must be ringing off the hook. They want a statement. Something to include in their articles. We had to draft a statement saying that we're taking this very seriously and looking into every possibility."

Janet raised an eyebrow.

"Well, now that this thing is national news, we may have to start paying more attention to it."

"Just so long as you don't get in the middle of my investigation," Janet said, stifling a laugh.

Ian winked, acknowledging her joke. He'd said some version of the same thing to her a dozen times, maybe more. "I'll do my best."

The initial clue that something strange was going on came when Janet didn't recognize the first two people who came into the café Thursday morning. The men wore skinny jeans and blazers with oversized scarves. Janet was pretty sure those were designer sneakers, and one had dark-rimmed glasses that said *Gucci* on the side. The other had a man bun and neatly trimmed beard. Janet was sure they weren't from around here.

"Oh, thank goodness there's somewhere in this town to get caffeine," the guy with the man bun said.

"Good morning," she said brightly. "What can I get you?"

"The biggest cup of coffee you have," the glasses guy said. "What do you want, Evan? It's on me."

"We both know it's on the company, Seth." The guy with the man bun—Evan—elbowed him playfully. "I'll have the same." He cocked his head to the side. "Do you have oat milk?"

"We do," Janet said. They'd been stocking it recently because a few people in town had dairy allergies.

His eyes widened, though Janet wasn't sure if it was delight or shock. "Oh, thank goodness."

"Can I interest you in any pastries? Or we have a full breakfast available."

Evan eyed the baked goods, but Seth scrunched up his nose. "Do you have egg whites?" he asked.

"Sure, we can do egg whites," Janet said. "Here's the full list." She handed him a plastic-coated menu.

"Just scrambled egg whites for me," he said, dismissing the menu.

"And I'll have one of those gorgeous chocolate chip muffins," Evan said. "Don't judge me. It was a long night."

"I had one of those myself this morning," Janet said with a laugh. "No judgment here."

"This place is cute," Seth said, turning around slowly while Janet placed a muffin on a ceramic plate. "It looks old."

"It is old," Janet said. "The station was built in the 1880s, and this was the original canteen."

"So cool," said Evan.

"Where are you from?" Janet asked.

"Los Angeles," said Evan.

Janet should have guessed.

"We just flew in on the red-eye," Seth said.

"What brings you to Dennison?"

"This is where that new Clark Gable movie was discovered," Evan said.

"We work for a streaming service in Hollywood, and they're very interested in acquiring that film," Seth said. "So we're here hoping to meet the owner. Do you know how we might get in touch with him?" He pulled out his phone and unlocked it, then squinted at the screen. "I think his name is Sam Watson?"

"That's right," Janet said. "He owns the theater." Janet decided it was best not to let him know that they had the footage locked up right here in the café.

"You can probably find him at the theater," Debbie added from the pass-through.

"And that's…where exactly?" Seth asked.

"Down the block, turn right at the corner. It's two blocks down," Janet said. "I don't know if he'll be there yet." It was just after seven.

"We'll try after we eat," Evan said. "Thank you."

Several regulars came in, and the morning passed in a rush of activity, but another group of people visiting from out of town arrived around midmorning. The two women wore heeled boots and big draped scarves, and the man with them wore a sweater with a garish colorful design woven into it. Janet might be wrong, but she guessed they weren't here just to see the museum and enjoy the small-town charm.

"Welcome to Dennison. What brings you to town?" Janet asked as she rang up their lattes. One of them had asked for oat milk. Janet made a mental note that maybe they needed to order more.

"We read about that missing Clark Gable film that was found here," one of the women said. "We're hoping to speak to the owner of the footage."

"Do you know where we would find him?" asked the other woman.

Janet told them the same thing she'd told the first group, and asked where they were from. They told her Los Angeles.

Ashling Kelly came in just before lunch, asking for a large coffee and a muffin to go.

"How's it going?" Janet asked. Ashling went to school and worked as a Jill of-all-trades to make money. "Keeping busy?"

"I've got plenty of projects, that's for sure," Ashling said. "I just helped Carson Argyle hang some pictures, and I painted a wall for Len Farnham. I also spent, like, a full day helping my grandma clean up her garden last week, but I don't get paid for that. So that, plus my schoolwork, keeps me plenty busy."

"I'm glad to hear it," Janet said. She picked up a paper cup and held it under the spigot of the coffee urn. "Hey, actually, Debbie and I were talking about your grandma yesterday. Do you know if she's around?"

"She's not going anywhere, at least not that I know of," Ashling said. "She's trying to finish up a quilt before Lauren Baglione has her baby, so I imagine she'll be at home a bunch the next few days. Why?"

"We were curious about something." Janet was being evasive, but Ashling didn't seem to notice or mind.

"I'm sure she'd be happy to talk to you if you stopped by," Ashling said.

"We'll do that," Janet said. She handed Ashling the paper cup of coffee. "It was good to see you."

"You too." Ashling held up the cup in a salute. "Say hi to Tiffany for me!"

"Seems like we have a number of visitors to town here to see about those film rolls," Paulette said after they closed up for the day. "I waited on two tables of people from New York."

"They must have hopped on the first plane after they heard, to get here that fast," Debbie said. "I suppose they're all trying to get the rights to own it?"

"That's what it seems like to me," Janet said. "Poor Sam. He probably wasn't prepared for the number of people I sent his way today."

"Poor Sam?" Paulette laughed. "Looks like he'll have a bidding war for the right to show that footage. I suspect he'll be just fine."

Paulette was right. Sam was probably sitting on a gold mine, judging by how interested people from Hollywood and New York were in the footage.

"Well, while he's sorting out the fate of those reels, I'm still going to try to untangle its history," Debbie said.

"Ashling said her grandmother would probably be around and happy to have visitors," Janet said.

"Colleen Kelly seems like a good place to start," Debbie said. "Shall we?"

They wrapped up a number of leftover cookies and drove to Colleen's house. On the way, Debbie told Janet that she'd gotten ahold of Gayle, who had invited them to come see her on Saturday.

"Works for me," Janet said.

Colleen was a retired schoolteacher who made incredible quilts that were displayed each year at the county fair. She lived in a bungalow-style home a few blocks from downtown. Snowdrops and daffodils bloomed triumphantly in the garden bed that lined the path, and colorful banners that said WELCOME SPRING decorated the front porch.

Janet knocked on the door, and a moment later Colleen stood in the doorway. She wore jeans and a blue wool sweater that was covered with small bits of thread, and her shoulder-length gray hair was pulled back into a messy ponytail. "Oh. Janet. Debbie. Hello." Her face broke into a smile. "Well, this is a nice surprise."

"We wondered if you had a moment." Debbie held out the plate of cookies. "We brought treats."

"That was good thinking, there." Colleen stepped back. "I can't say no to your cookies." She gestured for them to step inside. "I could use a break anyway."

Janet stepped in, with Debbie following a step behind her. "Ashling said you were working on a baby quilt?" Janet asked.

"That's right," Colleen said, closing the door behind then. "Lauren Baglione is due any day now, and her mother wanted something special for her first grandchild, so she asked me to help. Would you like to see it?"

"Please." Janet had never gotten too deeply into crafting, but she very much appreciated the skill and talent of those who pursued it. Colleen led them down the hall, past a TV room and a formal dining room with an antique pedestal table, and then into a bedroom that had been converted into her sewing room. A desk with a sewing machine was against the back wall, under the window, and plastic drawers of tools sat nearby. Inside the open closet door, Janet saw neat piles of fabric in a rainbow of hues. A high table lined the side wall, topped with rubber mats, rotary cutters, rulers, an iron, and all kinds of other tools. Blocks made up of blue strips of fabric were pieced together on the table. The strips were all different patterns and textures and shades of blue, which came together to make a pleasing design.

"She chose a rail fence pattern for this one, and I love how the fabrics she chose work together."

"It's beautiful," Debbie said.

"It will be once it's done," Colleen said.

"It's such a thoughtful gift," Janet said. "You do great work."

"Oh, I have fun. It keeps me busy." She led them out of the bedroom and into the living room at the front of the house. "Now, would you like some tea or coffee to go along with those cookies?"

Suddenly, coffee sounded delightful. They chatted about Ashling while Colleen quickly brewed a pot, and soon they were sitting in the living room, cups of coffee and plates of cookies in hand. The room was comfortable, with a rag rug over the wooden floor and overstuffed blue couches. Family photos and pictures of the sea lined the walls.

"Now, what was it you wanted to chat about?"

"Well—" Janet hadn't quite figured out how to broach the potentially difficult subject, and she was grateful when Debbie jumped in.

"Did you hear about the film that they found over at the theater?" Debbie asked.

"Oh yes. I read about that in the paper. It sounds very exciting, doesn't it? And to think it was there all this time."

"It is pretty exciting," Janet said. "We were lucky enough to be able to see the footage that Clark Gable shot."

"Were you now? That sounds amazing. What was it like?"

"Very interesting," Debbie said. "In the footage we saw, Clark interviewed several people from town about the war effort. Some of them are people who are still around. It was really neat to see Eileen

Palmer back when she was station master, and to see what it was like inside the canteen as they worked to prepare and hand out the lunches they gave away."

"It does sound very interesting," Colleen said. "Is there anything on it that explains what happened to the film? Who stole it and why?"

"That's a difficult question to answer," Janet said. Debbie jumped in and added, "That is, we aren't sure. There were also some things we didn't quite know what to make of in the film."

"Like what?" Colleen cocked her head.

"Well, there's one bit on the footage where Clark Gable is seen sitting in a booth at the old Delancey Diner."

"Grandma was a waitress there during the war," Colleen said. "She stopped when she had kids, but she used to always talk about that place."

"The thing is," Janet said. "Your grandmother shows up in the footage."

"She does?" Colleen's brow knit. "In the scene at the diner?"

"Take a look." Janet pulled up the video on her phone and slid the bar at the bottom to advance the footage.

"Oh my," Colleen said, gasping as the scene played out. "That's Grandma, and…oh, wow. She always did have plenty of sass. She's so young here."

"How old was she in 1944?" Janet asked.

"Goodness. She was born in 1927, so she would have been seventeen. Wow. It's so amazing to see her like that."

"We're interested in one thing she says in particular in the video, about money," Janet said.

"The line about getting money from other places?" Colleen said, and Debbie nodded. "I wondered about that when I heard it too."

"So you don't know what she might have been talking about?" Debbie asked.

"No. It might have been nothing," Colleen said, hope in her voice. "Just big talk coming out of her mouth when she was trying to impress the star?"

"It's entirely possible," Janet said.

"I don't know what else it could be," Colleen said. "Grandma did talk sometimes about how she'd wanted to be an actress once, but she certainly never mentioned anything about financing that dream."

Her voice trailed off. Janet's phone vibrated, but she didn't want to interrupt this conversation to check who was calling.

"Can I see it again?" Colleen asked. Janet tapped back into the video without checking her missed call icon. She found the scene and replayed it. It was a short segment, less than thirty seconds.

"I keep thinking, Grandma must have been so disappointed when this footage disappeared. She would have loved to have been in a documentary seated alongside Clark Gable," Colleen said. "But then I think she must be glad it never got out, or people might question what she was talking about there."

"Exactly," Debbie said, saying a lot without really saying anything.

"Oh." Colleen seemed to be processing their unvoiced thoughts. "You're wondering if she might have had something to do with it disappearing."

"We're just asking questions," Janet said. "We read a newspaper report that said there was a woman seen in the hallway outside Gable's room the night of the theft. Her name wasn't reported because she was a minor."

"Yikes." Colleen took in a long breath and let it out slowly. "What I know of my Grandma is that she was honest to a fault. But I obviously don't know if she was always that way. I honestly find it hard to imagine that she might have stolen this footage to cover up one thing she said about money. Even if that was in character, how would she have done it? How would she have gotten into the hotel room where it was kept?"

"We don't know," Debbie admitted. "It's entirely possible she had nothing to do with it. We're just asking questions."

Colleen took a bite of her chocolate chip cookie and chewed, and then set the plate down. "A bunch of Grandma's things are in the attic. I think there are some old diaries and letters and the like. I've never read through them. I wasn't ready after she passed, and whenever I think about it, I'm not sure I'm ready to go there yet. I'm not at that point in the grief process, and I guess it seemed…well, it seemed like invading her privacy somehow. But I wonder what might be in there."

"Would you be willing to take a look?" Janet said.

"I'll see what I can find," Colleen said.

They chatted for a few more minutes, and Colleen promised to let them know if she found anything.

"What do you think?" Janet asked as soon as they were back in the car. She turned on the engine, pulled her phone out of her purse, and set the purse on the back seat behind her.

"I think there must be a treasure trove of historical artifacts and documents in attics all over Ohio," Debbie said. "This is the second person who's told us they'll look through their parents' attic."

"I can't even imagine the things in my parents' attic," Janet said. "I think they have stuff up there from both sides of the family. It probably hasn't been looked through in years."

"You should check it out. Maybe there's something good hidden away."

"Maybe," Janet said dubiously. "Grandma was into collectibles, so who knows what I might find."

"Fair enough."

"Hang on." Janet looked down at her phone. "I have a voice mail from the police station."

"From Ian?"

"No." Janet shook her head and put the phone to her ear. The message started playing, and she recognized Veronica's voice. "Veronica."

"Hi Janet, we were able to dig up that old police file you were looking for, the one for the stolen film," Veronica said in her thick New York accent. *"If you want to come by, you're free to see it."*

"They have the police file," Janet reported to Debbie. "How do you feel about making a stop at the police station before we head back?"

"Sounds like a plan."

CHAPTER ELEVEN

"You're free to examine the file here, but it can't leave the station," Veronica said, holding out a battered brown accordion file. "You can use the conference room if you want."

"Thank you." Janet took the file and held it gingerly. She led Debbie into the back of the station and toward the windowed conference room. She waved at officer Brendan Vaughn, who looked up from his computer and waved. Officer Forest was at his desk as well. Ian must be in his office, but the door was closed so she couldn't be sure. Janet sat down in one of the chairs around the conference table, and Debbie sat next to her. Janet unwrapped the string that held the file closed. The hum of fluorescent lights echoed in the quiet room. The smell of must and dust wafted out as Janet pulled the sides of the file apart. She reached in and took out a packet of yellowed papers stapled together.

"This looks like the officer's report from the scene," Janet said, scanning the document quickly. It was handwritten in messy blue ink, but she could make out most of it.

"That hurts my eyes." Debbie squinted at the page.

"I'll read it out loud," Janet said. "These notes were taken by an Officer Michael Brennan at 11:15 p.m. on September 28th."

"That's the night of the theft, right?"

"It is," Janet said. "He says: 'A call came into the station just after 10:30 reporting a theft from a guest room.'"

Dennison, Ohio
September 28, 1944

Officer Michael Brennan did not know what all the fuss was about. Everyone seemed really excited about this petty theft, but for the life of him he couldn't understand why people were so distressed about a couple of missing rolls of film.

"Can you please show us the room where it happened?" Officer Meeter was saying to the hotel manager, who had placed the call. The call had come into the station just after ten thirty, and he and Officer Dan Meeter had responded to the Del Mar. He'd been hoping for a nice easy night, but no luck.

"Of course." The manager, one Bernard Williams, seemed to know Dan. "Come this way." He led them up the stairs and down a long hallway to a door marked 201. Bernard knocked, and the door opened, and a man with a mustache and dark hair welcomed them in. It was a big room, with a couch and table in addition to the bed and bathroom.

"Clark Gable," the man said, holding out his hand. His eyes were red and were brimming with fresh tears.

"Officer Brennan. Dennison PD." He nodded, but the guy was still holding out his hand. It was almost like he expected them to be impressed or something. And there Dan was, grinning at him like an idiot. What was it about this guy?

"Can you tell us what happened, Mr. Gable?" Brennan asked.

"Of course." He swiped his hands under his eyes, wiping away the tears. "I'm visiting Dennison filming a documentary, and when I went out tonight, I left the rolls of film I've shot since I've been here on this desk." He indicated a wooden desk next to the closet. "But when I got back, the film was gone. Someone must have come in while I was out and taken it."

"When did you leave the room, Mr. Gable?" Meeter asked.

"Around six. I went to the Delancey Diner for dinner and then to Sunshine Cinemas to catch the seven-thirty film."

"Can anyone corroborate your story?" Brennan asked.

The man hesitated a moment and raised an eyebrow. "Yes, I imagine one or two people might have seen me at both places. I'm sure if you ask around, you'll find out I'm telling the truth."

The cockiness of this guy was galling. Who did he think he was, so sure that people would have noticed him?

"What film did you see?" Meeter was asking.

"Arsenic and Old Lace. It was entertaining. Cary Grant is a good guy."

He decided to ignore this last bit. No way this guy knew Cary Grant. Brennan wasn't trying to call anyone a liar, but how much truth was in the rest of this guy's story?

"How were the film rolls stored?" Brennan asked. "They weren't locked up, just out on the desk for anyone to see?"

"My room was locked, so I didn't think I would need to put them anywhere special."

"You didn't use the hotel safe?" Brennan asked.

"I didn't realize I would need to take extraordinary measures to keep them safe in a sweet small town like this."

Didn't this guy know there was a war on? That there was crime everywhere?

"Was anything else out of place when you came back?" Meeter asked.

"My camera was moved. It was by the desk before I left, and it was on the table when I got back." He *pointed to a huge hulking machine on a tripod. "And my clothes appeared to have been rifled through."*

"Who knew about this documentary you were making?" Brennan asked.

"Oh. Well. A number of people, I think," Gable said. "I've been in town nearly two weeks working on it. I've met a fair number of people."

"Can you give me names?" Brennan was getting annoyed.

"It will take a while, but sure," Gable said.

"I think most people in town knew about the documentary," Meeter added.

Well, Brennan had never heard about it, so it couldn't have been that big of a deal. He would ask Meeter about that later. For now, he said, "Did you let anyone into your room this evening?"

"I did not," Gable said. "My key has been in my coat pocket all night."

"Can you think of anyone who would want to steal the footage?"

"No," Gable said. He brushed away tears again.

"What is your occupation, Mr. Gable?" Brennan asked.

"I'm an actor."

He couldn't have been a very good one. Couldn't even tone down the waterworks over some missing film.

Brennan and Meeter asked him some more questions and also investigated the room. There was no sign of forced entry. No visible evidence left behind. They dusted for fingerprints and grilled Gable on who all knew the film was here, and then were finally ready to leave.

"Please find those rolls of film," Gable said, tears in his eyes again. "I'm a veteran, a military man, and this footage is very important to me."

Brennan thought he was supposed to be an actor. Whatever. They'd do their best, he promised before finally, mercifully, leaving.

Debbie laughed. "Brennan doesn't have a clue who Clark Gable is, does he?"

"He must have been the only one in town who didn't know."

"I suppose some missing film doesn't seem like that big a deal unless you know who filmed it and why it was valuable."

Janet nodded. "That's it for that report," she said. "Let's see what else is in here." She set the paper aside and reached into the file.

"This appears to be the transcript of an interview," she said, pulling out the next stapled packet. It was neatly typed, and the time and date of the interview were given at the top of the page. At the back of the packet were several pages of what appeared to be random lines and dots made in blue ink. "And—oh wow. Is that shorthand?"

"Goodness." Debbie leaned forward. "It must be. But it just looks like a bunch of squiggles."

"This would have been before tape recorders," Janet said. "I guess that's how they took notes during interviews?"

"And then someone must have typed it up afterward," Debbie agreed.

Janet flipped back to the typed pages at the front of the packet. "This says it's from September 29, 1944 at 9:30 a.m."

"That's the morning after the theft," Debbie said.

"It looks like Officers Dan Meeter and Michael Brennan interviewed Bernard Williams. That's the hotel manager, right?"

"It is. I'd love to know what he has to say."

Janet set the paper down, and they both began to read.

Dennison, Ohio
September 29, 1944

Brennan didn't like the look of this guy, but he did his best not to show it as the hotel manager sat down.

"State your name and today's date," Dan Meeter said from his seat next to Brennan.

"I'm Bernard. You know that, Dan. We've known each other for decades."

"This is a police investigation, Bernie," Meeter said. "Please state your full name and today's date for the record."

Williams sighed. "My name is Bernard Williams, and it's September 29, 1944."

"For the record, Mr. Williams has declined to have a lawyer present," Brennan added.

"I didn't do anything wrong. I have nothing to hide. Dan knows I wouldn't steal from a hotel guest. Come on, Dan. Tell them."

"Let's get started," Meeter said.

"What do you do at the Del Mar, Mr. Williams?" Brennan asked.

"I am the General Manager. I make sure things run smoothly and the guests have an exceptional experience."

Brennan stifled a laugh. "That's quite a job."

"It's a good job. One I'm grateful to have, and that I can do with this bum leg."

Brennan gazed down under the table. "What's wrong with your leg?"

"Surely you noticed the leg brace, Officer Brennan."

"Please state it for the record, Mr. Williams," Meeter said.

Williams sighed. "A fever when I was five caused partial lameness in my right leg. That's the reason I'm not overseas fighting like I want to be. So you can skip that question. I tried to sign up, and the army wouldn't have me."

"We weren't going to ask," Brennan said. He hadn't said anything about wondering, though.

Meeter coughed. "Let's get back to your job. You said you make sure guests have an exceptional experience. What does that mean, exactly? What are your duties?"

"I greet guests at the front desk, I check them in, I hand out keys, I answer questions, I collect payment, I manage the other staff. I handle any problems that come up. I manage."

"Noted," Brennan said. "What about when you're not there? Who makes sure the guests have an exceptional experience then?"

"There is a night manager. Hernando Cortera. And Felice Marshall works on my days off."

"But you were on duty last night, correct?" Meeter said.

"That's right. I worked all day yesterday, and was about to wrap things up and go home for the night when Gable called the front desk to ask who had been in his room."

"Before we get there, can you tell us when you first met Mr. Gable?" Brennan asked.

"Of course. It was nearly two weeks ago, on September 18. That was a Monday. He walked into the hotel and asked for a room."

"Did you know who he was?" Meeter asked.

"At first I wasn't sure. He looked like Clark Gable. My wife loves to go to the pictures, so I've seen several movies he's been in. But you don't expect a Hollywood star to come walking into a hotel in the middle of Ohio, right? So I wasn't sure. But as soon as he started talking, I knew it was him."

"What did Mr. Gable say?" Brennan asked.

"He asked if there was a room available. I told him we had several and asked how long he would be staying. He wasn't sure but said probably a week or two."

"Did you ask him what he was doing in Dennison?" Meeter asked.

"I did not. The privacy of our guests is of the utmost importance to us. Of course I was curious, but I managed to keep it to myself."

Meeter shifted in his seat. "Do you typically ask guests to pay for their rooms when they check in?"

"As a matter of course, yes."

"But you didn't in this case, right?" Brennan asked.

"I did ask Mr. Gable for payment, but he told me he was waiting for his lawyer to wire over the cash. He promised he would get me the money the next day."

"And you gave him a room anyway, even though that's not the hotel policy?" Brennan asked. This guy was getting special treatment, that was for sure.

"I knew he had the money. He's a big star. It's not like he doesn't have the cash. I believed him when he said it would be wired to him shortly."

"Did your willingness to bend the rules have anything to do with Mr. Gable's celebrity status?" Brennan's wife had nearly choked when she found out who he'd spoken to last night. Then she gave him a full rundown of Clark Gable's greatest hits. Called him a dunce for not knowing. For a while there, he'd been afraid Marjorie would run off with him if given the chance. He knew who Clark Gable was now, that was for sure.

"You mean, did I break the rules because I was awed by his presence? No. What I did was recognize that having a celebrity in my hotel would be good for business."

"And was it?" Meeter asked. "Good for business?"

"I did notice an uptick of guests in the time he was at the hotel. I can't say for sure it was related, but there did seem to be a lot of people hanging around the lobby in recent days. I assume they were hoping to catch a glimpse of the star."

"Do you know why he chose the Del Mar for his stay?" Meeter asked.

"*I didn't ask, but we are by far the most upscale establishment in this town. The Del Mar is the only hotel someone of his stature might consider.*"

"*I see.*" Brennan stopped himself from rolling his eyes. "*Did Mr. Gable pay his bill the following day?*"

"*He did not. When I asked him, he said he was still waiting for his lawyer to wire over the money. He promised it would arrive soon.*"

"*How about the next day?*" Meeter said.

"*You already know the answer to that question, Dan. I told you at the Elks Club meeting two days ago. You know he never did get the money wired over.*"

"*You're right, Bernie. But I wanted to get it on record.*"

"*Fine. For the record, no, Mr. Gable did not pay his bill, even though I asked him each day of his stay.*"

Brennan said, "*There are reports that you confronted him about this in the lobby of the hotel.*"

"*Confronted is a strong word. When he left his room to head out for the day on Wednesday—*"

"*That would be the twenty-seventh?*" Meeter said.

"*That's right. By that time, he'd been here ten days without paying for his room, so as he was leaving the hotel that morning, I stopped him and asked him politely for payment. I let him know that he would not be able to continue on at the hotel without payment.*"

"How did he respond?" Brennan already knew but wanted to see what Williams said.

"He promised to pay me that day."

"Witnesses state that you then raised your voice and threatened him, saying that you were tired of his lies and that you would talk to the press about it if he didn't pay you," Meeter said.

"Selene wasn't even there when this happened. I don't know why everyone believes the story she's spreading."

Meeter checked his notes. "Selene McCauley is one of the maids at the Del Mar, is that correct?"

"She's your niece, Dan. You know very well she is."

"You dispute Ms. McCauley's story?" Brennan said.

"Look, I'm just saying, if anyone overheard the conversation, it was May, but she's not the one going around town telling everyone I threatened to throw Clark Gable out into the street."

"May is another of the maids at the hotel, correct?" Meeter looked down at his notes again.

"May Johnson. You know who she is. Her mother cleaned houses all over town, including yours. May was the maid who cleaned Gable's room while he was at the Del Mar."

"Do you think May told Selene what she over-heard?" Brennan said.

"I don't know. There were a few other people in the lobby at the time, and though I was being quite discreet, it's possible one of them overheard the incident."

"I see." Meeter flipped through his notebook. "It's been rumored that this is not the first theft at the Del Mar in recent years."

"There have been a few reports, as there would be at any place of business."

"Have any of the reports been resolved?" Brennan asked.

"I'm not at liberty to say."

"This is a police investigation, Bernie. You should say what you know."

"I'm afraid I have nothing I can tell you."

Brennan cleared his throat. "Okay. Did you know that Mr. Gable was storing the footage for his film in his hotel room?"

"I did not. If I had, I would have insisted he use the hotel safe. Something that valuable should never have been stored in a guest's room."

"What did you think he was doing with the film he was in town to shoot?" Meeter asked.

"I honestly didn't think about it. I do not pry into the private lives of our guests."

Meeter said, "When did you become aware of it?"

"Last night, when he reported it missing."

"Tell us about that," Brennan said.

"Like I said, he called the front desk and asked who'd been in his room. Well, May was the only one who had the key, and she was on turndown duty, so I said just the maid and asked why. He told me his film was missing and must have been stolen."

"What time was this?" Meeter asked.

"Sometime after ten. He'd only just come in for the night, and he went straight to his room."

"Let's back up," Meeter said. "Did you see Gable leave the hotel?"

"Yes, he went out around six. I didn't ask where he was going, but most nights he's been in town he's gone to the diner for dinner and then the theater. I assumed that was what he'd done once again, though like I said, I didn't ask."

"But you saw him leave the hotel?" Brennan wanted to be clear.

"Yes."

"Okay. And he came back around ten, you said. What happened then?" Brennan asked.

"He called the front desk and said someone had been in his room. His rolls of film were missing. I went to his room myself to investigate. He showed me where the film had been and that it was now gone. I called the police, and here we are."

"Can you tell me who had been inside the room while he was there? Who might have seen the film inside the room?" Meeter asked.

"The maids, of course. May, and Selene, and a few others over the weeks."

"Anyone else? You didn't go in and look around at all?" Brennan said.

"I did not. I would never."

"He's a big star. Anyone would have been curious."

"The insinuation is insulting. Dan, you can't possibly believe—"

"We're just looking for answers, Bernie. If you say you didn't enter the victim's room, I believe you. But was there anyone else you saw?"

There was a pause.

"You're awfully quiet, Williams," Brennan said.

"I did see a young lady." He swallowed. "She was coming down the stairs from the direction of Gable's room. I don't know what she was doing up there or how or when she got in. But I do know she wasn't staying at the hotel, and since she's a local kid, I thought it was odd."

"Who was that?" Brennan said.

"Helen McDonald. A teenager from town. I've known her family for years."

"Did you ask her what she'd been doing in the hotel?"

"I did, but she didn't answer. She just ran off."

"So you didn't see her go into or come out of any of the rooms?" Meeter said.

"No. I don't know how she would have without a key, and I don't see how she could have gotten one of those."

"You said you didn't see her come into the hotel?" Meeter asked.

"I did not."

"How did Ms. McDonald come into the hotel without your noticing, Mr. Williams?" Brennan asked.

"I was likely distracted by a guest when she entered. I always try to give every guest my full attention."

"So to be clear, you didn't see her come into the hotel, or go into or out of the room in question?" Meeter said.

"That's correct. I hate to think she had something to do with it. Her dad is a friend. But if we're looking for people who were acting strangely in the vicinity last night, she's certainly one."

Meeter met Brennan's eye. Brennan couldn't tell what he was thinking.

"All right." Meeter sighed. "Did you ever see anyone else go into or out of Mr. Gable's room?"

"I mean, the other Hollywood guy, his manager or whatever, Mr. Hallman, he took a room next door. Maybe he went into Gable's room. I don't know."

"Mr. Hallman's room was directly next to Gable's?"

"They're the two nicest rooms in the hotel. It only makes sense. I don't know if they ever visited each other in their rooms, though. From what I saw, Gable tried to stay away from Hallman."

"How so?"

"Hallman would wait in the lobby for him, and Gable would try to get past without speaking to him. I saw that happen a couple of times."

"Did you think that was odd?" It sounded odd to Brennan.

"A bit."

Meeter said, "Why do you think Mr. Gable was staying away from the producer?"

"I have no idea. I stay out of the private lives of my guests."

"Did anyone else have access to the key?" Brennan asked.

"There is one key the maids use. May was on duty last night, so she had it. That key gets you into all the rooms. The other copy is kept at the front desk. Of course, Mr. Gable had the room key."

"Did you leave the front desk at all last night?" Brennan asked.

"No. I was there all night."

"You never stepped away, not for a moment?" Brennan said. "A bathroom break, a snack?"

"I was there all night. No one else had access to the key."

"So if someone had access to the room, it would have had to have been someone using the maid's key?" Brennan said.

"Or Gable's own, I suppose." Then, he added quickly, "But you should talk to Helen. See what she has to say."

"Let's go back to the fact that Mr. Gable still had not paid for his room," Brennan said. "How much does he owe the hotel at this point?"

"Over a hundred dollars."

"And he still has not paid?" Meeter asked.

"He has not. Every time I ask, his lawyer is just about to wire the money."

"You were heard to threaten Mr. Gable the day before this incident, Mr. Williams," Meeter said. "You said he would be sorry if he didn't pay and that you'd get your money one way or another."

"We have already discussed that conversation. You can't honestly think I—I meant through legal channels. Banks, lawyers, that kind of thing. If we had to sue to get paid, we would. Just because you're a star doesn't mean you don't have to follow the rules."

"How much do you think that film is worth?" Brennan asked.

"I don't have the slightest clue."

"Michael, you don't really think..." Meeter let his voice trail off.

"We have to explore all angles, Dan. Mr. Williams, Mr. Gable is, as you say, a big star. There's a lot of people in Hollywood who would pay well for that footage he's shot."

There was a long pause.

"Cat got your tongue?" Brennan said.

"I would like a lawyer."

Janet set the papers down and looked at Debbie. "What do you think?"

"It seems Officer Brennan had figured out who Clark Gable was since the previous night."

"He had indeed," Janet agreed.

"So it could have been a maid, it could have been Bernard Williams, it could have been Helen McDonald, otherwise known as Helen Fletcher—"

"Helen was seen in the hotel, but she didn't seem likely to have a key."

"Right, but why was she there at all?"

"I don't know." Janet sighed. "Bernard—Bernie—is one of the few people who had access to the key, and he knew Gable was out for the night. And he got cagey when the officers pressed him on his threats to Gable."

"He asked for a lawyer, anyway. That must have been when he realized he was a suspect."

"Even being a fellow Elks member couldn't keep him from that, it seems."

"Did the interview ever get picked up again, once he had a lawyer?" Debbie asked.

Janet riffled the papers. "That's the end of this packet. Let's see what else is in here." She pulled out the next batch of papers, and they found it was a collection of short interviews with other guests who were staying at the hotel the night the film went missing. They read through them together. They were all pretty similar, as far as Janet could tell. None of the guests had seen anyone in the hallway leading to Gable's room. None had seen anything unusual. One guest, a Nathan Lannister, claimed to have seen a suspicious man loitering in the lobby, but none of the other guest testimonies corroborated that.

"There was no sign of forced entry, right?" Debbie said.

"That's what the report said. The paper reported on that as well. But things had been moved around inside the room."

"It had to have been someone with access to a key."

"Which means hotel staff are the logical suspects."

"Or someone working with the hotel staff," Janet said. "It could have been someone else, but someone from the hotel let them in."

"Let's see what else is in the file. Maybe it will give us more clues about who."

"Good thinking." Janet reached into the file and pulled out another stapled packet. "It looks like another interview report," Debbie said, squinting at the page. It was neatly typed, but the ink had faded some and the words were light on the page. "With—does that say May?"

"May Johnson," Janet said. "She was the maid who was on duty that night."

"Okay," Debbie said, leaning forward. Janet handed her the paper. She was happy to let Debbie try to make that out. "It's dated September 29, 1944."

Dennison, Ohio
September 29, 1944

"Please state your name and your title," Brennan said.

"May Johnson. I'm a maid."

"Can you tell us about your whereabouts on the night of September 28?" Meeter said.

"I was at the hotel. I was on turndown."

"Did you enter the room of Mr. Clark Gable?" Brennan said.

"I entered room 202 at around 7:30 p.m., a while after Mr. Gable had left for the night."

"How did you know he'd left?"

"Mr. Williams called from the front desk and told me. He asked me to do turndown in that room since the guest was out."

"How did you enter the room?" Meeter asked.

"I used the master key. It was clipped to my apron, like it always is when I'm on duty."

"Is it normal to clean a guest's room at that time of night?" Brennan said. Seemed like a strange time to be dusting if you asked him.

"I wasn't there to clean. I was there to turn down the bed, lay out a robe and slippers, and place a chocolate on the pillow. I had cleaned the room earlier in the day."

"Did you see the film inside the room?" Meeter asked.

"I saw two or three metal film canisters on the desk earlier in the day. I didn't see them when I went back that night."

"Did you think that was odd?" Brennan said.

"I didn't think much about it at all. Guests move things around all the time."

"Did you ever touch the film canisters?" Meeter asked.

"No. I never touch a guest's personal things unless I need to clean under them, and in that case, I always put the items back where they were."

"So you never touched the film?" Brennan said.

"I had no reason to touch them. No, I did not."

"Who else might have gone into the room?" Meeter said.

"No one, really."

"There aren't other maids?" Meeter said.

"Sure. There are three of us. There's Selene McCauley, but she wasn't there that day. And Susie Allerdice called out sick so I was alone working a double shift."

"Who else had access to the key?" Brennan asked.

"I had it clipped to my apron all day. The other master key is kept at the front desk, so you would need to ask Mr. Williams about that."

"Had you ever interacted with Mr. Gable?"

"Yes, once I went into the room when I didn't know he was inside. He was very kind and said it was no problem."

Brennan looked over at Meeter. He didn't have any other questions.

"Is that all?"

"Yes, that's all for now, Ms. Johnson," Brennan said.

After the maid left the room, Brennan turned to Meeter. "Shady, right?"

Meeter nodded. "Wouldn't look us in the eye."

"And why was she so cagey?"

"I suspect there's more to her story."

"We've heard that they were trying to pin it on May," Janet said. "You can see them digging here."

"She does seem like the most obvious choice, doesn't she?" Debbie said. "She's the only one who could roam freely around the hotel and had a key. If Bernard had left the front desk, people would have noticed, but she was going into the guests' rooms anyway, so no one would have thought it was odd to see her entering or leaving Gable's room. Even if she was carrying something out of his room, no one would have blinked. If she put it in a bag, they would have assumed it was trash."

"But I can't see anything concrete to show if she's guilty or not," Janet said.

"I suppose if they had that, they wouldn't have an unsolved case on their hands," Debbie said.

"I guess you're right." Janet sighed. "There are more interviews here," she said, pulling out the next batch. "How about we divide and conquer?"

Debbie agreed, and they split the pile of interviews in half and each started reading. Janet saw the interview at the top of her stack and smiled. "There's a follow-up interview with Gable the next day."

"Lucky." Debbie stuck out her bottom lip. "I've got interviews with a bunch of people who were at the diner and the theater the night of the theft. I guess the police were trying to corroborate his story."

"That makes sense. Tell me what you find out."

Janet looked down at the transcript of the interview with Clark Gable. It was again conducted by Officers Meeter and Brennan. The time stamp at the top said September 29, 1944 at 10:30 a.m.

Dennison, Ohio
September 29, 1944

"Thank you for coming in to speak with us again, Mr. Gable." Brennan said.

"Of course. Thank you for your help. If there's anything I can tell you to help you find the film, I'm glad to do it."

"I know we spoke about this last night, but for the record, can you please tell us how you discovered the film was missing?"

"Of course. I went out about 6, 6:30 or so. I was planning to have dinner at the Delancey Diner and then catch the film at the theater in town. Arsenic and

Old Lace. *When I left the room, the film was on the desk in metal canisters."*

"Did you see anyone strange lurking around your room?" Brennan asked.

"No."

"There was a maid who came in to turn down your room. Do you know who she is?"

"May. Sure. I said hi to her a few times. She seemed very nice. Wait, you don't think she did it, do you?"

"She's one of the few who had access to your room," Brennan said. *"She admits she was inside the room last night."*

"She didn't do it. I'm sure of that. She is a sweet woman. Honest. She couldn't have stolen it."

"You seem to know her quite well, Mr. Gable," Meeter said. *"I thought you said you'd only said hi to her a few times."*

"That's right. But you can tell a lot about a person in a short interaction. She wouldn't have done this. Please don't waste too much time trying to see if it was her."

"Who do you think might have, if not May?" Meeter asked.

"I don't know. It's unthinkable."

"There have been reports that you had an altercation with the hotel manager over payment," Brennan said.

"That was just silly. I have been waiting on my lawyer to forward the cash needed to pay for my room. I'm good for it, it's just gotten tied up. I calmly explained to him that I'm a man of my word and he will get his money. He understood that."

"He didn't seem to think it was as calm as all that," Brennan said.

"That's unfortunate."

"Do you think he could have been behind the theft?" Meeter said.

"I wouldn't know. Though it doesn't seem like a very good business strategy, to be honest, stealing from a guest. He does appear to be a smart business-man, if nothing else."

"Is there anyone else who had access to your hotel room?" Brennan asked.

"No."

"No one else entered the room in the time you've been in town?"

"Not that I know of."

"The hotel management reports that a representa-tive from your film studio arrived in town last week," Brennan said.

"Freddie. Yes, he showed up a few days ago. Sent by the studio to convince me to come back to LA. He didn't have access to the room, though."

"How would you characterize your relationship with Mr. Hallman?" Meeter asked.

"Fine. Good enough. He's a nice man. Being here, he's just doing his job."

"What is his job?" Meeter said.

"He's been sent to get me to abandon the independent film project I'm working on and convince me to come back to Hollywood to make money for the studio. He's been doing his absolute best."

"Making that film disappear would be in his best interest, in that case," Brennan said. "With the film gone, wouldn't you be more likely to return to Hollywood"?

"Sure, but I don't know. He's just a kid."

"Mr. Hallman is 35," Brennan said.

"Is he? He always seemed a lot younger than that to me. But still, I don't see it."

"You're saying you don't think he's involved?" Meeter said.

"I don't see how he could have gotten into my room in any case. He didn't have a key. Plus, it's my understanding that he was ill last night."

"Ill?'

"With a stomach bug. Or something he ate. I don't know. All I know is he didn't want to go out, and he told me he was going to ask a maid to bring up some medicine for his stomach."

"So Hallman was in the hotel room next to yours last night?" Brennan said.

"Presumably."

"And a maid brought him medication?" Meeter said.

"May was the maid on duty, so I expect it was her."

Brennan made a note of this on his notepad. Then he looked back up. "Do you know Helen McDonald?"

"Doesn't ring a bell."

"She's a waitress at the Delancey Diner." Brennan tried to read him. If he was lying, he was good at it. Then again, Brennan now knew he was an Academy Award-winning actor.

"Oh yeah. That cute one, with the blond curls? Wants to be an actress?"

"Miss McDonald is blond, yes," Meeter said.

"What does she have to do with this?"

"You didn't see her at the hotel at any point?" Meeter said.

"Why would she be there? She's a kid, and she lives here in town, right?"

Brennan was not about to answer his questions. But he had one of his own. "Who do you think might have taken the film, Mr. Gable? Every suspect we suggest couldn't have done it according to you."

"I honestly couldn't say. But you two seem sharp. I'm sure you'll figure it out." He paused. "This is such a nice small town. I never thought..."

"You never thought what?" Meeter asked.

"Well, it's just a shame, is all. Things here are not what I thought."

"I'm sorry to hear you're not enjoying your time here," Brennan said.

"Please don't take that the wrong way. Dennison is great. It's just... it's probably time for me to leave anyway."

"You're not planning to continue with the film you were making?" Meeter said.

"I don't think so. After this, my heart just isn't in it."

"What will you do instead?" Brennan asked.

"Probably head back to LA. Freddie will be glad, that's for sure. Make some more movies. See what happens, I suppose."

"We'll do our best to find the film for you, Mr. Gable," Meeter promised.

"Thank you."

Janet read through the transcript again, searching for clues she might have missed the first time. Was Gable right that Hallman had been ill in his room that night? Surely the police had looked into that. Maybe that was here somewhere. If May had brought him medicine, had she also opened the room next door for him? She had denied any involvement, though. Hmm.

Gable didn't seem to know who Helen was or what she'd been doing at the hotel. Janet couldn't explain it either, but she was missing something, surely. Was there an interview with her? Maybe in Debbie's bunch?

By this time, Debbie had finished reading through her packet and was looking at her.

"Anything useful?" Debbie asked.

"Maybe," Janet said. She told her what Gable had said about Frederick Hallman and about Helen McDonald Fletcher.

"Interesting. Because Hallman was interviewed in my batch."

"Oh, really? What does he have to say for himself?"

"He says he was 'indisposed' the night of the theft."

"Meaning what?"

"I take that to mean he was sick, which would corroborate what Gable says. He says May brought him medicine."

"May didn't mention that in her interview."

"No, but that interview might have happened before Hallman's, so maybe they didn't know to ask her about it."

"Interesting." Janet thought for a moment. "He had a strong motivation—he had been sent by his studio to get Gable to give up the project and return to Hollywood. Which he did, shortly after this."

"He's at the top of my suspect list," Debbie said. "Even if we don't know how he got into the room, he was right there, in the room next door, when the film canisters were taken."

"Has the book he wrote arrived yet?"

"It's supposed to show up tomorrow," Debbie said. "I'll let you know if he confesses once I get my hands on it."

"Wouldn't that be something?" Janet said.

"It would make this all a lot easier," Debbie said. "Though it doesn't seem likely."

"Is there anything else interesting in the interviews you read?"

"Gayle Zink was interviewed. She saw Gable at the theater after the show that night."

"That's right. Ray said she had." Then Janet added, "Saw him doing what?"

"Walking down the hall."

"Highly suspicious."

"Exactly." Debbie laughed. "She's funny, because she seems so young in her interview."

"She *was* young." Janet did some quick math in her head. Gayle was seven years younger than Ray, which meant she must have been around twelve or so at the time. That's about how old she looked in the footage.

"Yes, but it's funny that you can tell that by reading her words."

"How about we switch, and you see if there's anything I missed, and I'll see if there's anything you missed?" Janet suggested.

"Sounds good."

They switched packets, and Janet bent her head down over the yellowed pages. Debbie was right that Gayle seemed very young in her interview.

Dennison, Ohio
September 29, 1944

"You say you were at the theater last night," Brennan said to the kid.

"Yes, sir. The seven-thirty show." She kept her eyes cast away from her dad, who sat in the corner, arms crossed over his chest, his lips pressed together. Brennan didn't know what the story was, but the girl was in trouble with her father, that was clear.

Brennan asked, "What was playing?"

"Arsenic and Old Lace. It's a dark comedy about a man who discovers his elderly aunts are killing people."

"That's quite an adult topic for someone your age," Meeter said.

"It was all in good fun."

"Did you enjoy the film?" Meeter asked.

"I enjoyed Cary Grant. He's one of my favorites." She giggled. "Then again, it was hard to watch the screen knowing that the biggest star in Hollywood was right there in the theater."

"So you saw Mr. Gable at the show?" Brennan said.

"Oh, sure. We all pretended not to, but he's why half of us were there in the first place. We were all

hoping to catch a glimpse of him, maybe catch his eye. It would be like something out of a Hollywood movie, wouldn't it?"

"I'm sure I wouldn't know," Brennan said.

"Can you tell us about when you saw him last night?" Meeter said.

"Well, I was running late because I had to clean up dinner. Mom is doing poorly these days, so I do most of the cooking and cleaning. The show was about to start by the time I got there, and you had to go in this other door to get to the auditorium. The old one is closed now. So I was confused and rushing, but it wasn't hard to see where Clark was sitting, because there were people all around him. Anyway, Millie had saved me a seat, so I went over and sat by her near the front."

"Millie is...?" Brennan let his voice trail off.

"Millie Gulley. My friend I was meeting at the theater. She saved me a seat near the front."

"Did you stay in the theater for the whole show?" Meeter asked.

"Yes. We never leave before the end of the credits. We were the only ones left in the theater by the end."

"What happened after that?" Brennan asked.

"Millie went to use the restroom, and I hung out by the curtain waiting for her. And, lucky me, I got to see Clark again."

"You saw Gable by the curtain?" Meeter asked.

"Not the one at the front of the theater, the one by the concession stand. He smiled at me, and I couldn't wait to tell Millie. He was leaving the theater, and I wanted to follow him and strike up a conversation, but just then Millie came out of the bathroom, and by the time she'd caught up with me and I'd told her what had happened, he was gone."

"So to confirm, you saw Gable both before and after the show?" Brennan said.

"That's right. And he smiled at me afterward. I tried to catch his eye during the show, but Millie whispered at me to stop turning around."

"Did you notice anything else? Anything out of the ordinary?" Meeter asked.

"How much do you think it costs to get to Hollywood?"

Debbie was right—Gayle was so young. It was funny to see her that way in these pages. Janet supposed they'd all been young and immature once. Janet read through the other interviews in the stack, but she didn't see anything else worth noting.

Debbie looked up a few minutes later. "Did you find anything?"

"I don't think so."

"Me neither."

"There isn't an interview with Helen Fletcher. Not that I've seen, anyway," Janet said.

"Good point. I wonder why that is?"

"I imagine the police tried to get one. Maybe there's something here. Let's see what else is in this file." Janet pulled out another stack of other papers, but they appeared to mostly be summaries, reports giving updates on the progress the police had made on the case. Or lack thereof, honestly. There was a packet of papers from when a new police chief started in 1946 and the case was reopened, and another from 1953, when the investigation was taken up again, but there never seemed to be any real advance.

"Well, that was a whole lot of nothing," Janet said with a sigh.

"Not nothing." Debbie took out her phone and used it to take photographs of each of the pages. "We learned a few things: one, that Frederick—Freddie—Hallman was in the hotel, potentially with a way to get access to the room at the time of the theft."

"That last part is a stretch. We have no reason to believe May had anything to do with him or would give him access to Gable's room."

"Fair enough. But we know he was there, at least. And we also know Bernard Williams said Helen Fletcher was there, though we haven't heard from her why."

"Also that Bernard Williams was at the front desk the night of the theft, and again, the idea that this is not the first theft that's happened at this hotel in recent years," Janet added. "Which suggests a pattern. Something not quite right at the hotel."

"Bernard is also clearly friends with one of the police officers who investigated the theft," Debbie added.

"Do you think that colored anything about the investigation?" Janet asked.

"I would hope not, but I guess you never know."

"And we learned Gable was spotted at both the diner and the theater," Janet added. She looked over the stacks of papers and sighed.

"What's wrong?" Debbie cocked her head.

"I was hoping seeing the police file would answer some questions. Instead, it just seems to have raised more questions."

"The answer is out there somewhere," Debbie said. "We'll just have to keep looking until we find it."

CHAPTER TWELVE

By Friday morning, it was clear that news of the rediscovered footage had brought more visitors to Dennison. Janet counted half a dozen groups from out of town over the course of the morning. She chatted with each group and discovered that they came from either New York or LA, and it wasn't too hard to guess who was from which. The New Yorkers wore black, and the Californians didn't have real coats. Janet had never seen so many people wearing dark-framed glasses nor had so many requests for avocado toast.

Evan and Seth were back around midmorning, and Janet asked how their visit was going.

"That guy Sam was really nice," Evan said as he tapped his phone to pay for his oat milk latte. "He said he doesn't know what he wants to do with the film yet, so we're just going to keep trying."

"We want to take him out to dinner," Seth said. "What's the nicest restaurant around here?"

"You're standing in it," Debbie called from the kitchen.

"Well, duh, but you guys aren't open in the evenings," Evan said. "What about for dinner?"

"Probably Buona Vita," Janet said.

"The pizza place?" Evan grimaced.

"It's very good," Janet said. "It's very authentic Italian food."

"So many carbs," Seth said, shaking his head. "We'll have to go for a long run this afternoon."

"Good luck," Janet called as they walked away.

Harry, seated a few seats away at the counter, laughed and took a bite of his toast almost gleefully.

A little while later, another group walked in. A woman with curly blond hair and dark glasses over perfectly groomed eyebrows gazed at the menu. She wore a black dress and boots, and a man in a black leather jacket stood next to her. New Yorkers, then.

"Good morning. What can I get for you?" Janet asked, smiling.

"I'll have a latte," the woman said, setting the menu down.

"Just a regular latte?" Janet expected her to ask for some kind of nut milk or turmeric.

"Just a regular latte," she said.

"Make that two," said the man next to her.

The woman winked conspiratorially. "You must be so sick of all of us already."

"We're glad for the business," Janet said, "and to meet some interesting folks. Where are you all from?" Janet put the odds at fifty-fifty for Manhattan versus Brooklyn.

"Brooklyn," she said. "I'm Annie. This is Ravi." She bobbed her head at the man next to her.

"Nice to meet you. I'm Janet." She rang up the two lattes and waited while the girl tapped her phone against the card reader. "Welcome to Dennison. Are you here because of that Clark Gable film too?"

"I think that's why we're all here." Ravi smiled. "Those guys are from a streaming service." He nodded at Evan and Seth. "I used to work with the younger one. Those guys over there"—Ravi gestured at another group of Californians at the corner table—"are from a celebrity gossip show. I also saw a group from a Hollywood studio in town last night. We come up against them a lot for projects. They're good dudes."

"So the other groups are your competitors," Janet said.

"Sure, but they're also our friends," Annie said. "It's a small industry."

It didn't seem like it to Janet, judging by how many teams were here.

"Did you talk to Sam as well?" Janet poured milk into the metal jug and turned on the steamer.

"We met with him," Ravi said. "He told us that he doesn't know what he's going to do with the film yet."

"He could have something pretty big on his hands," Janet said.

"Looks that way," Annie said. "The thing is, no one has actually seen the footage. We don't even know if it's real."

"It's real," Janet said. "I can tell you that for sure. It's the real deal."

"Have you seen it?" Ravi's eyes widened.

"I have," Janet said. "It's definitely Clark Gable in the footage."

"Oh wow." Annie let out a gasp. "I would so love to take a look."

"You'd have to ask Sam about that," Janet said.

"He said he doesn't even have the film in his possession," Annie said. "So we checked in with the police in town, and they said they don't have it. Everyone keeps saying it exists, but no one seems to know where it is."

Janet's antennae went up. They were probing. No way was she going to tell them that the film was right here in the café.

"I'm sure it's being kept safe," she said, holding out two steaming cups of coffee. "I hope you enjoy your day."

"Thank you." Annie smiled, Ravi nodded, and they took their coffee and headed out. Janet watched them go. She knew they wanted the film. All the visitors to town seemed to. But it felt like these two had crossed a line, though when she thought about it, Janet couldn't say how. She just had the sense she had to be careful, suddenly.

The day was busy, as Fridays nearly always were, and several of the groups visiting town came back for lunch. When it was time to close, Janet was pleased to see the day's tally. They cleaned up and sent Paulette home, and then Debbie said, "I got a message from Colleen Kelly this morning."

"And you're just telling me this now?"

"We were busy, and you were distracted by the visitors."

"They can't all think they will get the footage, do they?"

"I bet not. That's why they're anxious to get in good with Sam, so he'll pick them." Debbie was quiet for a moment. "What do you think he *will* do with the footage?"

"I imagine he'll probably sell it to the highest bidder. That's what I'd do with it, probably. It would go a long way toward getting the new theater up and running." Janet set down the bottle of cleaning spray. "Anyway, what did Colleen say?"

"She found her grandmother's diaries in the attic. She asked if we want to take a look. She read some of them and thought they might help."

"Helen Fletcher's diary?" Janet said. "Why, yes we would like to look."

"Oh good. Because I already called her back and said we'd be there around three."

"In that case, we'd better get going."

They got in Janet's car, and as she was pulling out of the lot, Debbie said, "Huh."

"What do you mean by 'huh'?"

"There's a man sitting in a car over there." She gestured to the other side of the parking lot. "He was there when I came in this morning."

"What? Are you sure it's the same guy?"

"I'm sure."

"Why would he be sitting there this whole time?"

Debbie shook her head. "That's a very good question."

Colleen greeted them at the door, a wide smile on her face. "Good afternoon. Please come in." She stepped back to usher them inside. She had big glasses on, and her hair was in a messy bun with knitting needles stuck through it to hold it in place.

"Did you finish the quilt?" Janet asked as she stepped inside.

"Just barely. Lauren went into labor last night, and Margaret was able to bring the quilt to the hospital to meet the little guy this morning. Matthew Brett Baglione." She closed the door behind them.

"That's wonderful news." Janet made a mental note to send a gift to Lauren.

"I almost didn't finish it, truth be told," Colleen said. She gestured for them to follow her, and she led them past the formal dining room into the kitchen, where warm oak cabinets and dark granite counters were set off by a wallpaper border of farm animals that ran around the top of the room. "Once I went up into the attic, I got distracted by so many neat things. The boxes of my mother's old stuff were there all right, but so were trunks from my grandparents as well as my own kids' baby clothes and toys. I got so into an old photo album of my kids when they were little that Ashling had to come up and see if I'd hurt myself or died up there."

"Attics can be like that," Debbie said with a laugh.

"Anyway, I dug through the boxes of Grandma's stuff, and I found this," she said, gesturing toward a black leather diary on the wooden table. "It felt kind of invasive at first, since I don't think she ever intended for anyone to read what was there. But I found it interesting, and I think you will too." She picked up the diary and handed it to Debbie, who took it.

"Do you want us to read it here?" Debbie asked.

"Oh, no. You can take it," Colleen said. "I trust you'll keep it safe."

"We certainly will," Janet said. "Thank you."

"I hope it helps," Colleen said. Janet tried to read her expression, but Colleen wasn't giving away anything. She'd obviously read it and knew whether it implicated her mother or not, but they would need to wait until they got somewhere else to see what it said.

"We'll return it soon," Debbie promised, and they walked out of the house and back to the car.

"Where to?" Janet asked when she'd turned on the engine. Warm air began blasting out of the vents.

"How about the library?" Debbie said. "We can sit at one of the tables and read it. There are a few things I wanted to look up anyway."

"Sure thing." Janet put the car in gear. "No peeking while I'm driving."

Debbie had already opened the diary's cover, and she closed it quickly. "I would never."

Janet laughed. "What do you want to look up at the library?"

"I was hoping to try to learn more about Freddie Hallman. His book arrived, and I started reading it yesterday."

"Ooh. What did you find out?"

"It's pretty self-aggrandizing."

"He wrote and self-published a book about himself. That's not all that surprising."

"Fair enough. Well, he spends a lot of time talking about his childhood, about how hard he had it with a working mom and a dad who drank, but somehow he's always the hero of every story."

"It *is* his book…"

"I know, I know. Anyway, I skimmed all the stuff about how many girls wanted to date him in high school and read the part where he moved to LA to work in the film industry. He doesn't seem to have wanted to be an actor, but got a job reading scripts. He talks about how quickly his talent was recognized and how fast he moved up, how he married the prettiest actress on the lot, and soon he was working for the head of one of the big studios."

"Who did he marry?"

"A woman named Loretta Himmelman. She was in a few films in the thirties. I've never heard of her, but then I've never heard of most of the actors from this era."

"And what was his job?"

"He calls it talent management. I don't know exactly. He seems to mostly spend time having lunch with the actors, trying to convince them to take certain roles, based on what I've read. Each studio had actors on contract back in those days, and it sounds like his job was to get certain actors to say yes to certain roles in films the studio was making."

"I see," Janet said, though it was still a little vague. "What does he say about Clark Gable?"

"He mentions him several times. He claims to be the one who discovered Gable and got him to sign a deal with the studio."

"Is that true?"

"I have no idea. He also claims responsibility for getting Gable the part in *It Happened One Night.*"

"How nice for him." Janet didn't know enough about these things to tell whether this could possibly be accurate. "Does he mention his trip to Ohio?"

"Indeed. He talks about 'the Dennison episode.' The way he tells it, the studio sent him to get their biggest star to give up his solo project and come back to LA to make more movies."

"That part seems to align with what really happened, at least."

"Right. Small-town Ohio was not to his taste, though. He has some choice words to describe Dennison—"

"I don't want to know."

"The way he tells it, he came to town, got a room at the best local hotel, which wasn't up to his standards, and he worked hard to convince Gable. Finally, he was successful, because he was so good at his job, and Gable went back to Hollywood."

"Did he mention that the film Gable was shooting went missing?"

"Yes, briefly. It was a huge news story in that day, so naturally he talks about how he was here at the center of it all."

"At the center of it?"

"Not like that. The way he tells it, he was one of the few who knew all the players, and he was instrumental in giving police the clue they needed to solve the case."

"But they didn't solve the case."

"That doesn't appear to bother him," Debbie said. "He seems to think he gave them the slam-dunk clue. According to Hallman, he was in his own room next to Gable's, and when he went out for ice around eight that evening, he saw the hotel manager in the hallway outside of their rooms."

"The hotel manager? Not a pretty blond teenager?"

"No mention of a teenager. Just the hotel manager. He says Bernie was close to their doors, as if he was just entering or exiting one of them. Hallman says that Bernie started when he came out of his room and was surprised to see him, and though he tried to play it off like it was totally normal, it seemed suspicious. But he didn't think too much of it until afterward, when he learned about the theft. That was when he decided Bernie must have been either entering or coming out of Gable's room when he surprised him."

"That's strange. This interaction didn't come out in the police interview, did it?"

"It did not." Debbie shook her head. "Which may mean Bernie chose not to mention it for some reason at the time, or that it didn't happen."

"So that's an interesting question," Janet said. "Is the story true, or was that a fabrication added later?"

"If it was made up later, I presume the goal was to cast suspicion on someone else so that no one questioned whether Hallman had some role in the theft?"

"That's what I would assume." Janet sighed.

"Bernard insisted in his police interview he didn't leave the front desk all night."

"Which means one of them is lying."

"Hallman also says something I don't know how to interpret at all. It's small, but it stuck out as strange to me. When he's talking about getting Clark back to Hollywood, he says—" She bent over and pulled the book out of her bag. "Hang on." She flipped to the right page. "Okay. He says, 'Clark was heartbroken when he had to scrap the project, but I was never one to miss an opportunity.'"

"An opportunity for what?"

"He doesn't say. He just goes on and talks about his promotion."

"With no context?"

"That's why it stuck out to me as well. I don't know if it means something big happened but he didn't want to implicate himself, or whether it's just some throwaway self-aggrandizing statement. There are a lot of them in the book."

"It could mean he took advantage of the opportunity to steal the film, or it could mean…what?"

"I don't know. It's frustrating, but I wanted to flag it."

"I'm glad you did. Is there any way to find out more about what he meant?"

"He's long gone. Died of a heart attack in 1982. But he had children. That's actually why I wanted to go to the library. I was thinking I might see if I could track down his kids and ask if they could tell us anything. He had two sons, and they were alive when this book was written."

"Which was when?"

"1972."

"So, fifty-plus years ago."

"They were in their thirties then, so it's entirely possible they're still around."

"Eighty is the new forty," Janet said. "I guess it's worth a shot." She supposed it couldn't hurt, though his kids must have been very young at the time of the theft, and they would have been in California, not Ohio. She doubted they would be able to tell them much, even if they could be located, but it couldn't hurt to try.

"There's one more piece of information I found interesting," Debbie said as they pulled into a parking space in front of the library.

"What's that?"

"Hallman was promoted when he got back to Hollywood. He was given a big raise and a new title. He talks about it as a long-overdue recognition of how valuable he was to the studio, but the timing, just after he claims to have single-handedly convinced Gable to return to LA, is very strange."

"That is strange." It could be a coincidence. Maybe. Or it could be that Hallman was rewarded for taking extraordinary measures to get the studio's biggest star to come home. "You think those two things are related."

"It does make you wonder whether there's a connection."

"It does indeed." Janet pushed open the car door. "Let's go see what we can find out."

They were halfway to the library when Janet's phone rang. She pulled it out and glanced at the screen. *Sam Watson*. She answered the call on speaker so Debbie could hear.

"Hi, Sam."

"Hey, Janet." Sam sounded winded, and judging by the noises around him, he was walking outside. "Look, I don't know if this matters to you or not, but I wanted to let you know I got a certified letter from the Clark Gable Estate, claiming ownership of the film we found."

"Oh. Wow."

"Yeah, I've put a call in to Patricia Franklin, and she's going to help me sort this all out. I know you've met so many of the visitors to town and you have the film. It may change things, or it may not, but I just wanted to let you know."

"Well, that's an interesting development," Debbie said when Janet ended the call.

"Right. It appears there's one more party who wants to get their hands on the film."

"And this one might have the law on their side."

CHAPTER THIRTEEN

*E*llie Cartwright greeted them when they walked inside the library. They chatted with her for a few minutes about her plans for Easter, which was a few weeks away. "Catherine found a recipe for buffalo blue cheese deviled eggs she wants to try," she said, referring to her daughter, who was in high school. "I don't see what's wrong with plain old deviled eggs, but I'm willing to give it a shot."

Easter. Yikes. Janet hadn't given much thought to what she'd serve for Easter yet. But Tiffany would be coming home for the weekend, so that would be nice.

After they walked away from Ellie, Janet and Debbie conferred for a moment, and they decided that Debbie would use the computer terminals to try to track down Frederick Hallman's children, while Janet would take a seat at one of the long tables and read Helen Fletcher's diary. Then they'd come back together and share what they'd learned. Debbie sat in front of one of the computers, and Janet wandered over to the tables and found an empty spot. At the end of the table, a teenage boy was hunched over a math book, a steady beat pounding out of his oversized headphones, and he didn't seem to even notice when she sat next to him.

Janet set the diary on the table and opened the leather cover gently. The spine cracked as she looked down and saw the name

Helen McDonald Fletcher written in blue ink on the first page. The name Fletcher was written in an ink that was a slightly different color blue, and it made the name sit off-center on the page. Janet guessed that had been added later, after she'd married.

Janet gently turned the yellowed pages until she came to the first entry, written in March 1942.

> *Mother gave me this little book and said it would be a good place for me to write down what I'm feeling, so here goes. I don't know that it will help, but now that Dad has joined up and gone overseas to fight, I don't have anyone to talk to. Lenore annoys me more each day, always talking about her grades and how smart she is, and the boys are just obnoxious. Molly is sweet, but she's too little. Mother doesn't really listen, not like Dad does, so who knows, maybe this will be like having someone to talk to.*
>
> *Things have changed in town in just a few months. I didn't know Pearl Harbor would affect things here so much, but now the little town of Dennison is hopping with trains coming through all the time. It seems so strange that I'm expected to still show up at school and do math like nothing is different when the world has changed. I pray Dad comes home soon. I really hope this war is over quickly.*
>
> *Helen*

She must have still been in early high school in the spring of 1942, Janet realized. Which would track, if she was seventeen when Clark Gable came to town.

The next few entries were also about school and how much she missed her dad. Helen attended a Catholic high school—it had closed many years back, but Janet remembered it—and thought the nuns were strict but liked her friends. She thought reading was boring but liked music and art, and math was impossible. Helen was the oldest of many siblings, though Janet wasn't exactly sure how many there were in the family. She had to shoulder more of the responsibility with her dad gone and her mom stretched so thin. She was starring in the school's production of *You Can't Take It With You* that May, and loved being on stage.

> *April 3, 1942*
>
> *It snowed today. Only a little, but still. In April! I can't wait to get out of this town. After graduation, as soon as I get the money together, I'm going to California. I'll never have to wear a coat, and I'll become a famous actress, and I'll never have to deal with Ohio or Lenore nagging me about picking my things up off the floor ever again.*

> *May 25, 1942*
>
> *Billy Fletcher was hanging around with me and Melody today. I've been seeing him more at the soda fountain, and I realized he's actually gotten pretty handsome. I hadn't noticed, because it's Billy, and I've known him since we were kids, plus he's three years older than me, but he has that dark hair and he has muscles now, from football I guess. I thought maybe he was hanging around us because of Melody, but today he asked me if I wanted to go to the movies with him.*

Obviously I said yes. We're going to see Tortilla Flat *on Friday. I wonder if he will try to kiss me? Do I want him to? I'll report back.*

Over the next few entries, she talked more about her first date with Billy, which seemed to go well, and then a few more dates. He'd kissed her on the third date, behind the theater, and she was over the moon about it.

October 17, 1942

Billy's gone and joined up. I suppose he had to, and ever since he graduated, people have been asking him when he was going to. His dad needs him at the shop, but I guess he felt like his country needs him more. Or I guess he finally felt the pressure from everyone in town, and I get that. I mean, we need Dad too, but he's over there doing his duty, so why not Billy? Anyway, he joined the navy, and he'll be shipping out in a few weeks.

Over the next six months, she talked about Billy some, but he largely faded from the pages as she talked about school projects and her friends and how annoying her sister Lenore was. With her dad overseas and so many mouths to feed, the family needed her help, and she was excited to get a job as a waitress at the Delancey Diner in the evenings. In addition to helping feed the younger siblings, she was putting money aside to go to California. She also talked about the movies she went to at the Sunshine Cinemas, and how she wanted to become an actress someday.

Then, Janet noticed a new name start to come up. Wallace. When Helen mentioned Wallace, she always seemed to be meeting up with him after work, which didn't strike her as odd at first. If Wallace was a boyfriend, it would make sense that she would see him then. But there was something in the way she mentioned him in the diary that made Janet think he wasn't a boyfriend. Then, there was this entry, in June 1943.

> When Wallace came to the park after my shift tonight, he only gave me half of what he usually gives me for the same amount of stuff. I told him that was no good, that I wasn't going to do the trade, but of course I did. What was I going to do with loaves of bread and butter and coffee beans? Mother would want to know where it came from, and I would be stuck. I don't know if I'm going to keep it up. It's almost not worth it. But then I close my eyes and I see that Hollywood sign, and I think I probably will do it again.

Well, that was interesting. What was all this about? Was she… selling him food? But not food she could tell her mother about, apparently. Janet read on, and over the course of the next six months, there was enough context for her to piece together the story. Helen was taking food—was it leftover food? Helen never said—from the diner and selling to Wallace, whoever that was. What Wallace was doing with the food was also unclear. Probably reselling it, Janet imagined, but she couldn't say for sure. No one at the diner seemed to notice the food going missing, which Janet assumed meant either they didn't keep great inventory records or that she was taking small enough quantities that no one noticed. Janet wondered how much could go missing from the storeroom at the café before they would notice. A little butter here and there, a bag of coffee beans? She might not pick up on that for a while.

This, then, was no doubt what Helen had meant about money coming from places other than tips. She was stealing from her employer and profiting from the stolen goods. It couldn't have been much at a time, but after a year and a half, it would add up.

Lenore almost found my hiding spot for my Hollywood stash, Helen wrote in April 1944. *She was poking around under my bed when I came into the room. She said she was only looking for her slipper, but I don't think that was true. I moved it from under the bed to the top shelf in the closet. She's so short, she shouldn't be able to get it there.*

In September of 1944—Helen would have been a senior in high school at this point—she first mentioned seeing Clark Gable come into the diner.

September 21, 1944
Everyone in town is talking about how Clark Gable is here, but I still didn't believe it when I saw him walk into the diner. Martha seated him in my section, and I very nearly spilled soup all over him, I was so nervous. HE IS SO HANDSOME. He was so kind and so charming, and he left a big tip, and he promised to come back tomorrow night if I would wait on him again. I can't believe it. I think if I died tonight I would die happy.

September 22, 1944

Clark Gable came back tonight, and he told Martha he wanted to sit in my section. I almost screamed, but I kept my cool. He was definitely *flirting with me. What if he likes me and takes me back to Hollywood with him?*

September 24, 1944

Clark Gable was there again tonight. I'm beginning to think he's coming just to see me. After we closed up, he wanted to walk me out, but I had to go meet Wallace. I had potatoes in my pockets, so I had to say no. Curse Wallace and his stupid store. I should stop giving him stuff to fill up his shelves. I should have skipped the meet-up tonight and let Clark walk me home.

The next night, Helen wrote about the interview with Clark in the booth at the diner.

I'm going to be in a movie!!! I can't believe it. Maybe this is my big break. Maybe Clark really will take me with him. He chose me out of anyone to be in his film, didn't he?

The only thing is, I said something I shouldn't have. I let my big mouth go on about how tips aren't the only way to make money, which was SO dumb. Maybe no one will notice that bit?

September 26, 1944

Shoot, now I'm so worried about what I said in that interview I could barely sleep last night. That was so stupid!!

What if Martha sees it? What if anyone sees it? Maybe I can get him to edit that part out?

September 27, 1944

I was going to ask him to cut that part from the film, but he didn't come for dinner tonight. I will get in so much trouble if it comes out what I've been doing. Mom and Dad could be in trouble. What if I go to jail? Oh man, I wish that stupid film had never happened. I wish it would just go away.

September 28, 1944

Clark came to the diner again tonight, but he didn't stay long. He wasn't his normal self when I took his order. He wasn't flirty or fun or any of the things he normally is. When I asked him what was wrong, all he would tell me was that filming didn't go as he'd hoped today. I didn't have a chance to ask him to get rid of that part of the footage. So I decided to take matters into my own hands. It was probably dumb, but what else was I going to do?

That was it. There were no more entries for two weeks.

After reporting breathlessly on Clark Gable's movements and visits to the diner, she didn't report on the film going missing or his departure from town. Janet flipped through the pages, looking for more, but there wasn't anything more about Gable or about the film.

Which was odd. She couldn't help but think Helen wouldn't have simply stopped reporting on it unless... Well, she didn't know. But it didn't look good.

September 28 was the night of the theft. What had been going on with Clark that night? Had he had some interaction that had upset him or made him worried about the film in his room? Did he have a run-in with Frederick Hallman or with Bernard Williams? Did he know his film was in danger?

More importantly—had Helen stolen the film? She'd been spotted in the hotel, coming from the direction of his room. Had she gotten into his room somehow—but how?—and stolen the film?

It sure seemed plausible, based on what was here. Janet had to tell Debbie. She got up and walked over to the row of computer terminals.

"Find anything good?" Janet asked, taking a seat at the empty terminal next to her.

"A whole lot of nothing," Debbie said. "I used the genealogy site to track down his kids, and the older son passed away, but the younger son is alive. Raleigh Hallman. He lives in California. I did a deep dive into him and found that he's a lawyer who represented cigarette companies in their fight against acknowledging their product causes cancer."

"Lovely."

"He has plenty of money, though. He still lives in a big house up in the Hollywood hills. I found an email address for him. We'll see if he writes back."

"What did you say to him? 'Hey, I wanted to ask if your dad stole film from Clark Gable to get himself a promotion more than seventy years ago?'"

"Exactly." Debbie nodded. "That's precisely how I phrased it."

Janet grinned.

"I told him I was researching his father and his important role in the film industry in the forties. I figured a little flattery about how important his dad was would go a long way."

"No doubt."

"That's as far as I got. I found a number of newspaper articles from the forties and fifties, including one from the *LA Times* that talked about the theft and quoted Frederick as saying he was devastated by the loss of this important work."

"So we know he was lying about that," Janet said.

"Right. Since his whole job was to get Clark to abandon 'this important piece of work,' it seems doubtful he was sad about it. But that was the only article that was even remotely interesting as it relates to the theft. Let's hope the son comes through." Debbie leaned back in her chair. The wood creaked beneath her. "How about you?"

"You have to see this."

Janet told Debbie what she had learned, and Janet read her the relevant pages in the diary. "Oh wow," Debbie said. "Do you think—"

"I don't know, but it does seem like it's possible."

"It seems more than possible. This is practically an admission of guilt."

"I wouldn't go that far. But it doesn't look good for her."

"Right. So now, we've basically narrowed it down to Freddie the studio executive, Bernard the hotel manager, May the hotel maid, someone at the movie theater, and the woman who was seen near the hotel room the night of the theft and basically confessed to it in her diary."

"That's the long and short of it," Janet said. "But if she took it, she held on to it for two years before putting it in the wall of the theater to get rid of it."

"She got married and stayed in town, right? So she was here two years later. Bingo."

"Maybe."

"I mean, what other conclusion is there?"

"Let's think about other possibilities. If Helen didn't do it—"

"Which she clearly did—"

"We have a few other people who are under suspicion the night of the theft. We know Freddie needed to get Clark to abandon the project and come back to Hollywood—"

"Mission accomplished," Debbie said.

"—and that he was at the hotel. Maybe could have talked his way into getting ahold of a key. And we know he later said he never misses an opportunity, perhaps with regard to stealing the film. But he also cast doubt on the hotel manager, who he says was outside Clark's room that night, which may or may not be true."

"Which brings us to Bernard Williams, the manager. He was heard to have threatened Gable over the bill not being paid. He had access to the key. So he had means and motive," Debbie said.

"And according to Frederick, Bernie was seen outside the door of Gable's hotel room the night of the theft. We don't know why, but there couldn't have been too many reasons."

"But that detail was in Freddie's autobiography, written many years after the fact, and with the express purpose of making himself look good. It was never mentioned in the police interviews. So we don't know how reliable that particular piece of evidence is."

"Fair enough," Janet said. "But also, there was a pattern of thefts at the hotel. Don't forget about that. Someone had been taking things from guests over the years, and we don't know who. He could have seen the film as payment, knowing how valuable it surely was."

"Here's what I don't get about that theory," Debbie said. "Bernard couldn't have done anything with the film, could he? Once it was reported stolen, it was national news. If he had turned up with the film to try to get someone to pay him for it, everyone would have known he was the one who stole it."

Janet cocked her head, thinking about this. "Maybe there was a black market for this kind of thing. Maybe he thought he could sell it to a collector who would be glad to have the film in their collection, even if it couldn't be shown."

"But it didn't end up with a collector. It ended up hidden in the theater."

"So either he couldn't find a collector, or he never intended to sell it in the first place. Maybe it was just a way to punish Gable for not paying for his stay."

"That seems like the weakest motive to me," Debbie said.

"Or maybe Bernard was a collector himself. Not of film, necessarily, but of various items taken from hotel guests over the years."

"But what happened to the other items in his collection? Why was it only the film that was found?" Debbie pulled in a long breath and held it for a moment, then let it out slowly. "I don't know. Maybe that theory doesn't hold water."

"Or maybe it does, and we just haven't figured out the missing pieces yet."

"We have one more suspect," Debbie said. "The police sure wanted to pin it on May the maid."

"But no one else seems to think she would do something like that." Janet drummed her fingers on the table in front of her. "No one's come out and said it, but the implication is that May was an easy target. She was a different social class than the other suspects we've considered."

"She's also the only one known to be in Gable's room the night of the theft, though," Debbie said. "So even if those things do factor in—which they may or may not, we have no way to know—it's not like they just picked someone random to target. May *was* in the room."

"And she says the film was already gone when she went in to turn down the bed."

"Still…" Debbie shook her head. "I'm trying to be objective here, but it's pretty hard to discount what we just learned about Helen."

"I'll keep reading the diary," Janet said. "Maybe there's something more later that helps explain it."

"Maybe." Debbie narrowed her gaze. "Or we should just accept that we've found our thief."

CHAPTER FOURTEEN

*J*anet was up late Friday night, typing in the recipes she'd collected and arranging them using the software the online publishing company provided. By the time she went to bed, she had a draft of the book laid out and had pulled up a photo of the café to use on the book cover. She was getting there. Would Debbie like it? Was it the kind of thing people would want to pay money for? She hoped so. But in any case, she had to get to bed.

Saturday mornings were usually busy at the café, but on this day, there was a line forming before they'd even unlocked the door. The visitors to town seemed to have continued to multiply, though there were also several now-familiar faces among the crowd. Janet chatted with Seth and Evan as well as Annie and Ravi.

When two men in suits approached the counter, at first Janet didn't think anything of it. More visitors from one of the coasts— New York in this case, she guessed.

"Welcome to the Whistle Stop Café. What can I get you?" Janet asked.

"We are the legal representation for MGM Film Studios, the rightful owners of that film you have. You need to turn it over immediately."

"I'm sorry. What?" Janet couldn't have heard them right.

"That film belongs to MGM. You need to turn it over immediately."

"No it doesn't," Janet said, even as she faltered. Did she have the right to refuse? Could it really belong to these men? Why else would they be here?

"Hang on," Debbie said, coming over from the dining room. "Don't do anything, Janet. I'm calling Patricia."

"You are in possession of stolen goods," the first man said, crossing his arms over his chest. "If you turn it over now, the consequences will be less onerous for you."

Janet didn't move. She waited as Debbie called Patricia. "What makes you think the film is here, anyway?"

"We are very good at what we do," one of them said, and didn't elaborate. Janet didn't know what to make of that. Were they being watched? Was this place bugged?

"Patricia says don't do anything," Debbie called. "She's on her way."

"I'm afraid I can't comply at the moment," Janet said to the men, trying her best to keep her smile intact. "But can I get you some coffee or fresh-baked pastries?"

"It will be better for you if you turn over the stolen goods now," the second man repeated.

"Our lawyer is on her way," Janet said. "In the meantime, if you could step aside so I can help the next customer, I would appreciate it."

The men grudgingly stepped a few feet to the left, standing in front of the display of vintage candy and gum. Janet made an oat milk latte and a skinny cappuccino for two other customers, and a few minutes later, Patricia came rushing into the café, her coat flapping behind her.

"Is this them?" Patricia said, pointing to the two men in suits.

Janet nodded. Their attorney friend reached into her pocket and pulled out a business card. "I'm Patricia Franklin, legal counsel for these women. I'm told you've come in here demanding the missing film. Can I please see the adjudication?"

"MGM is the rightful owner—"

"That's been decided in court, has it?" Patricia said, raising an eyebrow. "My understanding, based on the laws and statutes of the state of Ohio, is that the property in question is rightfully owned by the party who owns the land on which it was found. The statute of limitations for the loss of this film has long passed, if it ever belonged to MGM in the first place, which it did not. And there is already another legal claim on the property in question, which puts this squarely into the category of contested property. Do you have a different understanding of the laws of this state?"

"That film is the property of—"

"You can come back with an order from a judge that says that," Patricia said. "Until then, you are trespassing on private property and are being asked to leave."

Neither man moved.

"Or we can have you removed if you prefer. Ms. Shaw's husband is the chief of police in this town," Patricia said, nodding at Janet. "Don't think he won't race down here the moment we call him. Now please leave."

The men stood, seemingly frozen for a moment longer, and then turned and walked out of the café without a word.

"That was impressive," Debbie said quietly as soon as both men had left the café. "I'm a little bit afraid of you now."

"What she means is thank you," Janet said.

"I'm glad you called," Patricia said. "The nerve of them, coming in here to ask you to turn over the film."

"I didn't know what to do," Janet said.

"That was their hope," Patricia said. "They wanted to scare you into turning it over. They had no legal right to ask you to do so, though, at least not one that's been established."

"Is what they said true?" Debbie asked. "Is there any chance the studio does own that film?"

"I highly doubt it," Patricia said. "It's more likely the Gable Estate owns it, if an outside party does. Though I believe we will establish ownership for Sam Watson. Still, a judge would need to determine that."

"You sounded pretty certain, invoking the laws of the state of Ohio," Janet said.

"Hey, I know my stuff. And it got them to go away, didn't it?" Patricia chuckled. "From what I understand, it was an independent project Clark Gable was working on, wasn't it?"

"Yes, but he was under contract with the studio," Debbie said.

"I suppose it would depend on the terms of that contract, and whether its terms were in effect in perpetuity, and what the law says about ownership."

"So you're saying it's not as simple as 'finders keepers'?" Debbie said.

"Maybe not. But if they did stake a claim, it would take a lengthy and expensive court case to prove it. In the meantime, there is no reason to give it to them." Patricia glanced toward the windows, where they could see the men conferring quietly outside. "I think you should find somewhere more secure to store the film, though, just in case. Maybe at the police station or in a safe-deposit box."

"We'll tell Sam that we can't keep it here any longer," Janet said.

"And you'll want to let Ian know what happened, so he's aware," Patricia said. "In the meantime, feel free to give me a call if you have any more trouble."

"You better believe we will."

Sam came over a little while after that and took the film, saying he was going straight to the bank to put it inside a safe-deposit box. Janet felt better knowing the film would be safer—and that they would be too—but part of her was sad to see it go. There was something kind of fun about having it in the café.

After they closed up, Janet and Debbie climbed into Debbie's car and pulled up directions to Gayle's home in Columbus. The drive would take just over two hours, and they came prepared with lattes and cookies for the road.

Gayle Bailey lived in a yellow one-story Victorian-style home in a quiet, tree-lined neighborhood by a large park. The buds on the trees were just beginning to emerge, and as Janet and Debbie walked up to the house, Janet thought how lucky Gayle was to be able to live on her own in her nineties. Gayle's daughter Trudy lived nearby and came around to help and check in every day, but Gayle still lived independently and even drove.

They rang the doorbell, and a few moments later Gayle opened the door, smiling at them.

"Well, hello. It's good to see you both. Thank you for making the drive."

"We're so happy to see you," Debbie said, stepping forward to give Gayle a hug.

"You look great," Janet added.

"Still kicking." Gayle laughed and ushered them inside. She led them into a living room with stained oak floors and high ceilings covered with pressed tin tiles. Big front windows let in lots of light, and a large marble fireplace stood against one wall. "Please sit. Now, tell me all about this Clark Gable film. I can't believe they found it after all this time."

"It's pretty incredible," Debbie said. "It was found in the old theater, but no one knows how it got there."

"Sunshine Cinemas," Gayle said, shaking her head. "I spent so much time in that old place, though that was mostly later. It wasn't like it is these days, where everything is a remake of something else and you can sit on your couch to stream it. Back then, going to the theater was an event."

"We heard you were at the theater the night the film disappeared," Janet said.

"That's right," Gayle said, a smile curving her lips. "And you better believe I got in trouble for it, didn't I?"

"You did?" Janet hadn't read this in the police report.

"Oh yes. I wasn't supposed to be there. I was only twelve, you see, and my parents, well, they hadn't actually said *not* to go see the pictures, but they made it clear they didn't much like the idea of films. They saw it as a waste of money, of course, but also, they were deeply faithful people, and the church looked down on it. They were from the generation who saw actors as morally suspect, so I think that had more to do with it than anything. Well, anyway, that was easy enough to overcome. Whenever there was a film I wanted to see, I met Millie there and stayed over at her place for the night. We always went together."

"You were naughty." Debbie grinned.

"I'm not proud of it, but that's what I did. Millie was the youngest of six, so her parents never cared what we did or where we went."

Janet had doubts that even parents with many children didn't care what their kids did, but she wanted Gayle to continue.

"So you and Millie went to the theater to see *Arsenic and Old Lace*?" Janet asked. It was amazing to be talking to someone who was there the night the film was stolen.

"Is that what was playing that night?" Gayle said. "I don't remember what it was, mostly because we weren't really there to see the film this time. We had heard that Clark Gable spent many evenings at the theater, and we were hoping to catch a glimpse of the star. Millie had the biggest crush on him."

"She was twelve?" Debbie asked.

"Millie was thirteen. She loved to lord it over me that she was a year older than I was. But she had two older sisters who both had crushes on him, so that was probably where that came from. She often did just exactly what her older sisters did. She even married the younger brother of her sister Ethel's husband, if you can believe it. Anyway, we went to the show, and it seemed like we weren't the only ones in town with the same idea, because the place was full. A lot of the women from town were there, and Clark himself was there too. Millie let out the loudest yelp when she saw him, and I was so mortified, but thankfully he didn't even notice."

"Where in the theater did he sit?" Debbie asked.

"The very back row. It was almost as if he didn't want to be noticed, though of course that was impossible. We were all looking for him. Well, Millie wanted to get right up close to him, but all the seats around him were already taken, so we had to sit at the front of the theater."

"It sounds like the theater was pretty packed," Janet said.

"It was. Once word got out that was where he spent his time, lots of people were suddenly interested in going to the movies. Anyway, I kept turning around to sneak peeks at him until Millie told me to stop. It's no wonder I don't remember the movie."

"How did Clark react to so many people gaping at him?" Debbie asked.

"It seemed like he didn't even notice, to be honest. I think he was used to it, wherever he went, and he'd learned to tune it out."

"Did he seem to pay attention to anyone in particular that night?" Janet asked.

"Not that I saw. He mostly just sat there and watched the film."

What had happened in the hotel while he'd been sitting there in the theater? Who had gone into that room and taken the film canisters?

"We read in the police report that you saw him after the show," Debbie said.

"That's right. Millie was so mad. She went into the restroom. She'd had a large Coke during the show, but I didn't have money for that, so I just waited outside, and I saw him walk right past me while I was standing outside waiting."

"What happened? Did he see you?"

"The theater was pretty well cleared out by then, because I liked to watch to the very end of the credits. Millie was itching to go because Clark had already left the theater, but I figured that there would just be a line for the restroom if we left right away anyway. Everyone always mobs the restroom as soon as the show's over. Anyway, when we finally left, we were some of the last people and the hallway was mostly deserted. Millie went into the restroom and I stayed there, in the hallway, and who comes walking down the hall but Clark Gable himself." She chuckled.

"Where exactly were you?" Janet asked.

"To the side of the concession stand, kind of? By the popcorn machine. There was this big curtain over there at that time, and you couldn't go past that, so I was there."

Janet tried to picture it.

"And Clark came from where? The bathroom was to the rear?"

Gayle nodded. "Toward the curtain. Away from the door."

"Did he see you?" Debbie asked.

"He did. He smiled and kind of ducked his head, almost like he was shy. Millie was so mad she'd missed it."

From the way she said it, Janet could tell it was still one of the moments Gayle looked back on fondly, even all these years later.

"What happened after that?"

"Not much. Millie came out, and by that time Clark was gone, so we left the theater and went to her house. We stayed up far too late, let me tell you. Millie made me act out the way Clark smiled at me probably a dozen times and tell her everything about what he was wearing. I described all the details, his hat and his bag and his coat, but she kept asking anyway. Then the next day the police came by our house looking to talk to people who had been at the theater, and at first my dad told them none of us had been there, but then they asked for me specifically. Boy, did I get in trouble. Mom and Dad were so mad. That was the last time I was allowed to stay over at Millie's house for a long time. I was so upset, thinking it was so unfair. Of course I got it once I had a kid. Poor Trudy never got away with those kinds of shenanigans, too bad for her."

Debbie was laughing, but Janet was thinking about what Gayle had said.

"Why did the police seek you out specifically?" she asked.

"I think they were just looking to verify Gable's story that he attended the movie, and since Millie had told her older sisters, who'd told everyone in town, that I'd seen him after the show, they wanted to hear about it from me. But I was happy to tell them about it—I knew how lucky I was to have had a personal interaction with him, no matter how small. Every woman in that theater was hoping for that, and it happened for me."

She was quiet for a moment, almost as if she was lost in her memories. Janet was still trying to picture the layout of the theater, trying to envision it, but couldn't make sense of what Gayle was saying. It didn't square up with what she'd seen of the layout.

"That wasn't the first time I'd met Clark Gable, though," Gayle said.

"It wasn't?" Janet asked, focused on Gayle once again.

"No. And the funny thing is, my mom asked me not to tell the police about that first time, so I kept it quiet. I actually don't think I've told anyone about it since then."

Janet looked at Debbie and saw the confusion she was feeling mirrored on Debbie's face. Hadn't Gayle just said her parents were very faithful people? Surely that meant they didn't condone lying?

"Can you tell us about it?" Debbie asked. She sounded tentative, but Janet could tell she was just as curious as Janet was.

Gayle was quiet for another moment and then shrugged. "They're all long gone by now. After all this time, I don't see what harm it could do."

CHAPTER FIFTEEN

Dennison, Ohio
September 28, 1944

Gayle looked up from her homework when she heard a knock at the door. Mom was in the kitchen cooking, and Gayle realized she wasn't going to get it, so she pushed herself up and stomped to the door. Why did she have to do everything around here?

But when she opened the door, she thought she was seeing things. Was that really Clark Gable on her doorstep? What was he doing here?

"Hello," Clark said. It truly was him. Gayle was going to explode. Wait until Millie heard about this! But then he went on. "Is Dolores Zink your mother?"

Gayle nodded, mutely. She couldn't get her mouth to work the right way to form sounds.

"Is she home?"

Gayle nodded again. Gayle and Millie had made plans to go to the theater that night because they'd heard he spent most evenings there. But here he was, at her house!

"Could I please speak with her?"

"Hold on." Gayle turned and walked away, and it wasn't until she was halfway back to the kitchen that she realized she'd left him standing on outside. He carried a large bag in one hand.

"Come in," she said, rushing back. Clark laughed, took off his hat, and stepped in through the open door-way. Gayle hurried to the kitchen.

"Mom, Clark Gable is here," she said.

"What?" Mother turned and wiped her hands on a dish towel.

"Clark Gable is here. He's in the hall."

Mother set the dish towel down, untied her apron, and draped it over a kitchen chair. How was she so calm? Why wasn't she keyed up about this? "I'll go see what he wants. You stay here, Gayle."

Then, she walked out to the hall. Mother had told her to stay in the kitchen, but she hadn't told her not to look, so she peeked around the corner and watched as Mother smiled at Clark Gable, and said, "Hello, Clark."

What was happening? Did Mother know him? Why was he here?

Mother said something quietly and then led Gable into the good parlor and closed the door. Gayle wanted to go listen at the door so badly. What was happening in there? She tried to focus on her homework, but she couldn't, not when Clark Gable was in her house. She finally gave in and got up to go listen at the door. Mother was talking, but she was talking so quietly Gayle couldn't hear what she was saying over the ticking of the grandfather clock. She went back to the kitchen and waited. A half hour passed. They were supposed to leave for her piano lesson soon. It was every Friday afternoon, and mother never let her skip her piano lesson. What was going on in there? More boring talking, she discovered when she listened at the door again.

More than an hour had passed when the door finally opened and they stepped out. Clark had his hat in his hand again, and his big bag in the other. Mother's eyes were red, like she'd been crying.

"Thank you," Clark said, and she walked him to the door. He waved at Gayle, sitting at the table, and then stepped out. Mother shut the door behind him. She stood there for a moment, her hand on the closed door, and then, slowly, she turned to Gayle.

"I need you to do something for me, Gayle," Mother said.

"What?" None of this made sense.

"I need you to forget any of that happened."

"Forget it?"

"Don't tell anyone you saw him here." Was Mother being serious? How did she expect Gayle not to tell Millie about this?

"Not even Father?"

Mother took in a long breath, and then she let it out slowly. "Not even your father."

That was when Gayle knew it must be important. Mother was honest to a fault. If she didn't want Father to know...

"Are we in trouble?"

"No, we're not in trouble," Mother said. "But I need you to keep this secret for me. Can you do that?"

Gayle didn't know what to say.

"Why?"

"I wouldn't ask if it weren't important. Please, Gayle?"

Slowly, Gayle nodded.

"When was this?" Janet asked. "You said you'd planned to go to the movie that evening?"

"Yes. It was that day. The film was stolen that night."

This story was unbelievable. "So what happened?" Janet said.

"I didn't tell anyone," Gayle said. "I knew it had to be important, so I kept her secrets."

"What was it about? Did you ever find out?" Debbie asked.

"At the time, I started to wonder all kinds of things. Mostly I wondered if he was my real father, which doesn't even make sense, because he was in Hollywood at the time I would have been conceived, and I look exactly like my actual father. There was absolutely nothing in their encounter to make me think there was anything romantic between them. But at the time I had this grand fantasy that he was my dad and I'd go to live with him in California and be a movie star too." She shrugged. "I was twelve. The truth is, I don't know. It's not like my mom stopped to explain to me what was going on. And I still don't know to this day."

"It must have been difficult to keep that secret," Debbie said.

"You better believe it," Gayle said. "The biggest star in Hollywood had come to our house, and I couldn't tell anyone? I really wanted to tell Millie—if she was excited about him walking past me at the theater, I knew she would lose her mind over him being at our house. But I didn't."

"Did you ask your mother why she wanted you to keep it quiet?" Debbie asked.

"Of course I did. But she wouldn't say. Then, when the police came the next day asking about being at the theater, she pulled me aside and told me not to say anything about Clark's visit to our home."

"But she didn't say why?"

"She didn't. I thought it was very strange. But once again, I promised her I wouldn't. I didn't know what was going on, but I knew it had to be important. I thought I was protecting her, I guess. I don't even know what from, but I thought she was saying she would get in trouble if anyone knew, so of course I didn't tell. Not even Ray." She was quiet for a moment. Then she added, "You're the first people I've ever told."

"And you never found out why?" Janet was grasping at straws, she knew. Surely Gayle would have told them what had gone on if she knew.

"I never did. Maybe she would have gotten in trouble if I'd told the police, but more likely that was just something a child worries about. I asked her one time, years later, toward the end. She was in the hospital with an infection, and I was asking her about her life, just different parts of it I didn't know about, and when I asked her about Clark, she just told me, 'You don't want to know about that.' When I insisted I did, she told me, 'It's a sad story. Best not to dwell on that.'"

"That's it?" Debbie looked as unsatisfied as Janet felt.

"She wouldn't say anything more. I've wondered over the years what she knew, but I've decided that whatever she and Clark talked about, she didn't know what happened to that film. She would have come forward if she had known, and not let poor May bear the brunt of the suspicion. So she didn't steal it or know who did. But she knew something."

"Did she leave behind any diaries or anything of that sort?" Janet asked.

"I'm afraid not. She wasn't the type to dwell too much on her feelings. I wish I knew how to help you, but I don't."

It was so tantalizingly close, yet too well hidden.

"What do you think happened to that film?" Debbie asked.

Gayle sat back, adjusting the throw pillow behind her. An orange striped cat came around the corner of the sofa and leapt up next to her. "I truly don't know. There was a Hollywood producer guy who was hanging around town after Clark showed up. Most people in town thought he was behind it. And maybe he was."

"It sounds like there's a *but* coming," Janet said.

Gayle smiled. "It's just that the older I get, the more it seems that people always blame the outsider, don't they? No one knew him, and he was this fast-talking city slicker, which made him easy to hate. But did that mean he stole the film?" She shrugged. "Maybe. Probably. All I'm saying is that I don't think most folks in town really thought about any other possibility, because he was easy to blame."

"Other possibilities like what?" It was almost like Gayle was hinting at something she couldn't say.

"Oh, I don't know." She rubbed the cat's head. "Sometimes folks just aren't all that creative, are they?"

"What do you mean?" Debbie said.

"Well, the police suspected May because she was in the room but also because she was an easy target. She didn't have what we would now call the social capital to fight back, I guess. And we all thought it was the Hollywood executive, because he was the outsider. We picked the obvious answer too, I guess."

"Is there something more you know?" Janet asked tentatively.

"No," Gayle said. "I would tell you, I promise. Just chalk it up to the ramblings of an old woman, if you want. It's just…wouldn't they have solved it, found proof, if one of the obvious answers was correct? I just can't help wondering if there isn't another explanation no one considered at the time."

Listening to her, Janet couldn't help but wonder if she was right.

CHAPTER SIXTEEN

We need to find out what happened in that good parlor between Gayle and Ray's mother and Clark Gable," Janet said as they rehashed the conversation on the way back to Dennison. "If it was important enough for her to ask Gayle to keep it from the police, it was very important."

"But what was it? How do we figure that out?" Debbie said.

"I don't know. Both people who were in that room are gone. Unless there is some record if it—"

"—and Gayle says there isn't—"

"—we can only guess."

Both fell silent as they sorted their thoughts.

"It's interesting that it was only after Gayle told us that story and admitted she'd never shared it before that she suggested there must be an explanation other than the obvious ones," Janet said.

"Just because Gayle thinks there might be another answer doesn't mean we chuck out the suspects we have," Debbie said. "She may be right, and we need to think about what other explanations we might be missing, but we shouldn't dismiss the possibility that one of our current suspects is behind it."

"You're right, of course. It still could be Bernard Williams, or Frederick Hallman, or May Johnson. Or someone connected to the theater," Janet said.

"But most likely it was Helen."

"Helen is a strong contender."

"And probably not May."

"Well, everyone who knows her seems to think not. But that's not evidence."

"Okay, fine. So we have several solid suspects, each with motive and opportunity," Debbie said. "But the police never found evidence that any one of them was guilty."

"And someone put it inside the wall of the theater two years later," Janet said. "So someone had it here in town all that time. Whether that was the same person who stole it is another question, though. The police never found the other explanation, if one existed."

"The police never found the film either, so we have an advantage there. We know where it ended up. We just don't know how."

"Right. So what else do we know that the police didn't?" Janet tried to think this through.

"We know the film was hidden at the theater, and we know when—during the 1946 renovation. But we don't know why, or who did it." Debbie was quiet for a moment, and then she gasped. "We know Clark had a secret conversation with Dolores Zink the day the film was reported missing, a conversation Dolores asked her daughter not to mention to the police. Wait." Debbie grabbed the handle of the car door and leaned forward. "Do you think Clark gave the film to Gayle's mother? Is that what Clark was doing there in the good parlor with the door closed? Asking Dolores to keep the film hidden for some reason? Was Dolores responsible for the film going missing and ending up in the theater?"

"Gayle said her mother wouldn't have kept quiet if she'd known where it was. She wouldn't have let May be accused if she'd known."

"You're right."

"Wait. Dolores had been a family friend, right? Isn't that what Ray said?"

"Of sorts. More like an employee, I think," Debbie said.

"Well, anyway, she knew the family. Maybe Clark needed someone he could trust, for whatever reason, and he sought out an old friend of his mother's."

"But why would he have given her the footage he'd worked so hard to make?"

"And if he gave her the film, how did it then end up in the theater two years later? Did she just hold on to it?" Janet thought back. "Besides, May said she saw the film canisters in Clark's hotel room on the day they went missing. So they weren't hidden in the Zink house."

"True. And if he'd given them to Dolores, why report them missing in that case?"

"This doesn't make any sense." Janet tapped her fingers on the steering wheel.

"Okay. Let's try another angle. Let's think about what happened at the theater that night," Debbie said.

"But what does that night matter, if the film couldn't have been put into the wall until the renovation two years later?"

"Well, we *do* know who else was at the theater the night the film disappeared. Someone who had direct access to the film."

"Clark Gable. But the film had to be put inside the wall during the renovation of the theater, and Clark was long gone by then. So he couldn't have put it there."

"Which is not the same as saying he couldn't have had the film at the theater at all that night," Debbie said. "We dismissed the possibility earlier, but maybe we were too quick to have done so. Maybe that's what Gayle was getting at. We know he had access to the film. Could he have left the film at the theater that night somewhere else, and it only made it into the wall later?"

"So, what, we think he took the film to the theater, lost it somehow, and then reported it stolen, and then two years later someone tucked it inside a wall?"

"I don't know. I'm just throwing out ideas based on what we do know. But let's just say the film wasn't stolen from his hotel room after all. Maybe he did bring it with him to the theater that night. Didn't Gayle say he had a bag with him?"

Janet nodded. "She did. And a hat."

"Those canisters would have been easy to slip into a bag of some kind. Maybe the film was actually stolen from him at the theater. Or maybe he brought it with him and threw it in a trash can, and someone found it there and kept it. Maybe it was in someone's possession for years before it ended up in that wall."

"But why would he report that it had been stolen from his room if it hadn't been?"

"Why would he do any of this?" Debbie said. "Why did he visit Gayle's mom in secret? Why did he come to Dennison at all? Surely there were lots of places in the country where he could have made a movie about the war effort at home. Why here? There's so much we don't know about that night and about that time in general. We may never know the answer to some of these questions. The police tried to find them for years and never could. But we do have one major advantage over the police in the 1940s, and that's that we knew the film ended up at the theater, and we know when. So let's focus on that."

"I see what you're getting at. Maybe we've been focused on the wrong thing. We've been so intent on finding out what happened at the hotel that night, but the police already investigated that thoroughly and didn't come up with anything. What we know that they didn't is that someone brought the film to the theater at some point, and that it ended up in that wall that was built in 1946. But we haven't spent much time asking where it was in those intervening years. Who could have had it all that time? The answer to this mystery is in how the film ended up in that wall."

"I think you're right," Debbie said. "How do we find that out?"

Janet was sure they were missing something. There was something there, just out of reach, that would help them make sense of it. What was it?

Finally, she shook her head and said, "Your guess is as good as mine."

Sunday morning dawned clear and cold. It was the kind of morning that made you feel like spring was just around the corner but still frustratingly unattainable. Janet dressed in a long skirt and sweater and topped it with a wool coat, longing for the days when she wouldn't need to bundle up just to walk to the car. At least Ian looked dapper in his dress shirt and slacks.

On the way into the church building, Janet spotted a man inside his car in the parking lot. Was that the same car they'd seen outside the café the other day? It was a black Ford. There were a million black Fords around here. But why was he just sitting there? He had a hat and sunglasses on too. Janet almost alerted Ian, but what was she going to say? There was nothing inherently wrong with sitting in your car. Why would he be following her? She was being paranoid.

Janet and Ian chose the pew behind Debbie and Greg, who were flanked by Greg's sons, Jaxon and Julian. They already appeared like a family. The service was lovely, and they sang "Great is Thy Faithfulness," one of Janet's favorite hymns. She appreciated the sermon on the Beatitudes, and she enjoyed chatting with members of the church family during coffee hour. But the whole time, she was unsettled, her mind swirling around, trying and failing to unearth a solution for how the film could have ended up in that wall two years after it was taken from Clark Gable's hotel room. Where had it been for those two years? Had Dolores Zink had it all that time? Had she hidden it in the wall of the theater during the renovation? Gayle said that her parents didn't approve of the theater. Then again, they probably didn't approve of lying either, and yet she knew Dolores had done so, or at least lied by omission to the police.

Janet needed to find out more about Dolores. That secret conversation in the Zinks' good parlor had to be the key to this whole thing. Gayle didn't know what had happened in that room, and

Janet guessed Ray didn't even know it had happened at all, given that he'd been overseas and Gayle had told no one. But Dolores must have known something. Janet would see what she could learn about Dolores Zink.

Ian had to go to the office after church, and Debbie was planning to have lunch with her parents. Janet had thought to spend the afternoon working on Debbie's recipe collection but decided to head to the library instead. A grant from the state had allowed them to stay open on some Sunday afternoons, and Janet was lucky that this happened to be one of them.

"You just can't stay away." Ellie smiled as Janet walked inside. The smell of lemon cleaner and old books greeted her.

"I can't," Janet said. "It's true."

"Anything I can help you find this time?" Ellie asked.

"I don't even know what I'm looking for," Janet admitted. "I'm just going to poke around in the databases for a bit, I think."

"Have at it. Let me know if you need help."

Janet promised she would, and then she settled in at the computer terminal and opened the database that gave access to the county clerk's records. Finding some basic information about Dolores Zink might not tell her what she needed to know, but it couldn't hurt. She did a search for the name *Dolores Zink*, and it pulled up only a handful of records. She was listed as the mother on both Gayle's and Ray's birth certificates, and the other record was her death certificate. Dolores Zink had died October 24, 1962, and was survived by her husband Hector, her children Ray and Gayle, and her father, Milton Hildebrand. There were no property records in her name, but perhaps Hector had purchased their home before they married. Using the name *Dolores Hildebrand*, Janet found the marriage certificate. Dolores Hildebrand had been married to Hector Zink on June 7, 1924. She also found a birth certificate for Dolores, who had been born in Uhrichsville on January 31, 1887.

That was all great, but it told her absolutely nothing about Dolores's relationship with Clark Gable.

Janet decided to try the newspaper archives to see if anything useful came up. She pulled up the archives for the *Evening Chronicle* and searched the name *Dolores Zink*, and again for *Dolores Hildebrand*. Aside from an announcement of her marriage, there was no mention of her in either name.

Janet was starting to think this was a fool's errand. Whatever she was hoping to learn about Dolores, she wasn't going to find it here. She sat back and tapped her fingers on the keyboard. Did whatever she was looking for even exist?

Dolores Zink—Hildebrand at the time—had worked for Clark Gable's mother, caring for the baby and the family when she was very young. She had later met in private with Clark, in 1944. She would have been fifty-six at the time, with her son off at war and a twelve-year-old daughter at home. That was all they knew.

What had happened in that room? Why had she told Gayle not to mention it? How did that omission affect what had happened after that? Janet didn't know. But it did give her an idea.

Maybe she was going about this the wrong way. Maybe what she needed to do was learn what had happened to the suspects after the story ended. After the suspicions had died down. One of them still held on to the film, or knew where it was. One of them was still involved, two years later.

She already knew that Frederick Hallman had returned to Hollywood, gotten promoted, presumably for his role in bringing back the studio's main star, and gone on to have a long and successful career in Hollywood. He'd had children. Debbie had reached out to his son, but she must not have heard from him yet, or she would have told Janet. Maybe they would hear from him soon, but by all accounts, Frederick had had a successful life.

But what about the others? It didn't take too much digging in the newspaper archives and county clerk's records to find out that May Johnson had married a Kirk Garland and had two kids with him. Their marriage and the birth of their two children were both reported in the newspaper. Her peach pie had won a blue ribbon at the county fair, and she'd passed away in 1979. That was all. Had she ever been to the theater? Did she have and hold on to the film until she could find a place to get rid of it?

Janet next searched for the name *Bernard Williams* in the archives and found an article about the closing of the Del Mar in 1963. Bernard had retired when the hotel closed its doors. Williams was quoted as saying he was "proud and honored to have welcomed thousands of guests" to the hotel. He had passed away in 1984.

Had he ever gotten paid by Clark Gable? She wondered….

She typed in the words *Del Mar Dennison* and found a couple of other articles. Most of the other pieces were the ones she'd already read, about Gable's film being stolen from the hotel. But there was one interesting piece she hadn't seen before.

GROUNDSKEEPER ARRESTED IN DEL MAR THEFTS, read a headline in the paper in 1946. The article reported that Malcom Hallowell, a part-time repairmen and groundskeeper, had been caught breaking into a guest's room and had confessed to dozens of other thefts over the years.

Hallowell was promptly fired, according to hotel staff, but Hallowell insisted that he was not responsible for the hotel's most famous missing item, rolls of film shot by Hollywood scion Clark Gable. "I had nothing to do with that," Hallowell insisted.

Janet wasn't sure what to make of this piece of news. Part of the reason Bernard had been a prime suspect was because of the many thefts at the hotel over the years. If he wasn't responsible for those, did it mean that he was now less suspicious? But then the man who was responsible for those other thefts insisted he hadn't taken the film. So where did that leave Bernard on their list of likely suspects?

Janet felt her frustration mounting. She had to be missing something. This puzzle had a solution. She just wasn't seeing it yet. Janet was becoming more and more sure the answers hinged on whatever had happened in that parlor between Clark and Dolores. But even without a record of what it was, there had to be some way to figure this out. There was a clue somewhere, if she could just find it.

The best way to find the solution was methodically. She would go back through everything she'd learned so far and see if she could spot anything she'd missed before. Janet went to the microfiche machine and pulled up the original newspaper articles she'd read, the ones published in the days after the theft.

Movie Footage Stolen from Gable's Hotel Room

Police received a call at 10:32 p.m. reporting the loss of the footage shot by Hollywood star Clark Gable. Gable, who has been staying in Dennison while shooting scenes for his upcoming documentary about the war effort on the home front, returned from the Sunshine Cinemas to find the film, which he'd kept on the desk in his hotel room, missing.

Janet read through the rest of the article, but nothing jumped out at her. She found the paper for the next day, and the next, and read each one carefully, looking for any clue that she'd missed before. But try as she might, she couldn't find anything that seemed to cast any new light on the disappearance.

There had been follow-up articles, she knew, and she scanned through the crowded pages of type until she found them again. It really was impossible to read these old newspapers. How did they manage to fit so many words on the front page? She tried not to get distracted by all the headlines and just look for the ones she wanted. Aha. Here it was. A month after the theft, there had been that article about how police were still investigating. She found that again, and read it, but it was exactly as unhelpful as it had been before. There was another one a couple months later, Janet was pretty sure. She scanned through the old editions until she saw it, and read it again, but still, just as she remembered, there was nothing new to report.

This was a waste of time. Janet was about to click off the newspaper page and give up when her eye caught on something. In the bottom corner of the page, there was an ad for Sunshine Cinemas. It said—

But that couldn't be right. She checked the date on this edition of the paper. November 28, 1944. But then why was…?

Janet picked up her phone. If what she was seeing was right— and she was pretty sure it was—then they had made a big mistake. She called Debbie. "We've been looking at this all wrong."

CHAPTER SEVENTEEN

W hat do you mean the theater was renovated in 1944?" Debbie asked. Debbie was driving home from her parents' place while Greg and the boys were headed to their house, and Janet could hear her blinker in the background. "It was renovated in 1946. That's what Sam said."

"That's what Sam told us. But that can't be right. I'm looking at a copy of a newspaper from November of 1944, and there's an ad for the newly renovated theater. The ad says, 'Now with two screens for twice the film fun.'"

"Okay, first of all, that's a terrible line of advertising copy, but secondly, how can that be true?"

"Sam must have been wrong about the date of the renovation, I guess. That's the only explanation. Because according to this ad, the renovation was completed in 1944."

"Does that mean that the theater was being renovated the night the film was stolen?"

"It may. And if it does—"

"Then someone who was there that night could have been responsible for the film getting put into that wall."

Neither one of them said what Janet knew they were both thinking.

"We need to find out for sure," Janet finally said. "I'll call Sam and see what he can tell me."

"Yes, do that," Debbie said. "Then call me back."

Janet noticed a few dirty looks from fellow library patrons, so she grabbed her coat and went outside to make the call.

"Hello, Janet," Sam said brightly.

"Hi, Sam. I have a quick question for you."

"Sure thing, What's up?"

"When you gave us a tour of the theater, you said the place had been renovated to add a second screen in 1946. Are you sure about that date?"

"Pretty sure. Why?"

"I found an ad in a newspaper from 1944 announcing the opening of the second screen at the theater," Janet said.

"Really?" Sam sounded as surprised as she was. "I mean—I could have sworn it was 1946. That photo from when they renovated says 1946."

"Your timeline was based on the photo?"

"Not just that. I thought I read…but you know, I don't know for sure, now that you bring it up. I sure thought it was 1946, but maybe I've got that wrong." After a moment, he added, "Can I see that ad?"

"Sure. I can print off a copy and send it to you."

"I'll dig around and see if I can find anything that gives the date in the papers I have. I would hate to have that wrong, and it would be nice to know for sure."

"Thank you," Janet said.

"If you're telling me the theater was actually renovated in 1944, it seems like that could make a big difference," Sam said. "That might mean the renovations were happening when that film vanished, doesn't it?"

"Depending on the timing, it could," Janet said.

"I'll see what I can find out," Sam promised.

"I'll do the same on my end," Janet said.

She hung up and called Debbie back. "Sam isn't sure. He was basing his knowledge on the date etched into one of the old photographs. So it's possible he has it wrong."

"We need to find out for sure," Debbie said.

"I can ask Gayle if she remembers. She recalls so much from that night, she might know that detail. I could also call Max Hersey," Janet said. "But he was going out of the country, so I don't know when he'd be able to get back to us."

"That would be great. But I know someone who can help us figure it out in the meantime."

"Who?"

"Can you meet me at Greg's?"

Greg. Of course. He dealt with the plans for and history of the building.

"I'll be there in a few."

Janet called Max Hersey as she drove. He might be able to tell them for sure. But his phone appeared to be off. No doubt he was in Italy without an international plan. Well, maybe Greg could help.

As she drove, she noticed a black Ford several blocks behind her on Third Street. Was she just seeing things? She turned quickly onto Spring

Street and drove slowly, waiting to see if the Ford made the turn too. When it drove right on past Spring without even slowing, Janet realized she was being paranoid. Why would someone follow her?

Janet parked across the street from Greg's house just as Debbie was getting out of her car. Greg's son Jaxon was in the driveway, practicing his jump shot.

"Nice one," Debbie called as Jaxon, a sophomore in high school, sank a clean basket.

Jaxon glanced their way and nodded, and then retrieved the ball and started dribbling again. "Hey, Debbie. Dad's inside," he called, his eyes focused on the ball.

"Thank you," Debbie said as she led Janet to the front door. Debbie rang the doorbell, and Janet realized it wouldn't be much longer before Debbie wouldn't have to knock. She would have a key, and would live here.

Julian, a sweet eighth grader with a dirty blond bowl cut, answered the door with Hammer, the family's border collie, at his feet.

"Hi, Debbie," Julian said. He had a handheld video game system in his hand. "I think Dad's in the kitchen."

Debbie thanked him and led Janet through the living room and into the kitchen, at the back of the house. They found Greg with his head under the sink, a wrench in his hand.

"You never get a day off, do you?" Debbie asked.

Greg scooted out from under the sink, and his face broke out into a wide smile when he saw Debbie. "At least I like the client in this case," he said. He set the wrench down and looked up at them. "The sink is leaking, but it's an easy fix." He sat up and dusted his jeans off. "To what do I owe this honor?"

"We have a question about the renovation at the theater," Debbie said. "Not the one you're doing now but the one from the forties."

"When they remodeled to add a second screen?" Greg pushed himself up to standing.

"Exactly. Sam told us that renovation happened in 1946, but Janet found an ad in the old paper advertising that the theater now had two screens from November of 1944."

"Huh." Greg wiped his hands on a dish towel.

"We were wondering if you knew," Debbie said.

"Not off the top of my head," Greg said. "I can look through the papers I have, but the plans from the Department of Buildings only show the theater in its most current configuration. They would probably have plans for the earlier renovations on file, though. Assuming the work was done legally and built to code, they would have had to file their plans with the Department of Buildings and make sure the finished work passed inspection before they could open. The files would have dates on them, for sure. The office is closed now, but I could look tomorrow, if you want me to."

"Could you? That would be wonderful," Debbie said.

"Sure. I'll go first thing, and I'll let you know what I find out."

Janet was looking forward to a nice dinner and then relaxing with a book and a cup of tea. It would be nice to rest tonight before the madness of a new week started. Ian's car was in the driveway when she got back. Good. He was home. She hoped things had gone well at the station and they would be wrapping up the drug case quickly.

Janet noticed a car parked in front of her house as she walked to the door, but she didn't think anything of it. This was a silver Mercedes—not the same car that she'd thought had been following her. But then the driver's side door opened and a man in a suit stepped out. Janet squinted. Did she know this guy? He was coming toward her and the house, though, with a brown accordion folder under his arm.

"Hello?" Janet said as he got closer.

"Janet Shaw?"

"Yes." How did he know her name?

"This is official notification that you have been named in a lawsuit. This folder contains the paperwork and information about when you'll be summoned to court. If you have any questions, please have your lawyer contact the office of Dial, Mercer, and Howe."

"Excuse me?"

But instead of answering, he only handed her the folder and walked away, hurrying toward his car. Just as he opened the car door, Ian opened the front door and stepped out.

"Who was that?" Ian asked, narrowing his eyes at the man as the door to the Mercedes slammed shut.

"Some lawyer or courier," Janet said, shaking her head. "I think I've just been served."

CHAPTER EIGHTEEN

*J*anet and Ian went inside and looked over the papers the process server had handed her.

"This says I'm being sued for possession of stolen property," Janet said. "The Hollywood studio is still claiming they own that film, and now they've filed a lawsuit to try to force us to turn it over."

"But Sam owns that film."

"That's what Patricia thinks. But the Gable Estate has claimed it too, and now the film studio has taken it up a notch."

"What a mess," Ian said. "I thought you didn't even have the film anymore?"

"We don't. Sam has it in a safe-deposit box at the bank."

"In that case, this should be easy to clear up," Ian said. "Maybe not for Sam but at least for you."

"I'll call Patricia." But before Janet had a chance to call her, her phone rang. Debbie.

"Did you just get served too?" Debbie asked.

"I did."

"I've never been served before. It was like something out of a movie. I didn't know that they did that in real life."

"Apparently they do." Janet sighed. "I was just about to call Patricia. Hopefully she can help us straighten this all out."

A few minutes later Patricia was on her way over, and so was Debbie, and all Janet's hopes for a nice quiet Sunday night had gone out the window. Janet cooked pasta while Patricia looked over both sets of papers, with Debbie seated next to her.

"It's pretty straightforward," Patricia said, finally glancing up from the papers. "They're suing you both for holding property they claim is theirs. But if you aren't in possession of the film, it should be pretty easy to get this dismissed."

In the back of her mind, Janet wondered if the person who had been watching her had somehow missed that the film had been moved, but she quickly dismissed that thought. No one was watching her.

"I can't believe they hired process servers at all and filed a lawsuit."

"Why not?" Patricia shrugged. "The studio probably has very deep pockets and a team of lawyers on hand, and they no doubt see the film as very valuable."

"But it's not even theirs," Janet said. "They can't just claim they own it."

"They're trying to make the case it is theirs," Patricia said. "Because Gable was under contract with the film studio. If they can get a judge to believe them, they could end up with it. I suppose they're banking on the idea that we won't fight them on it. But that's where they're wrong."

"So what's our next step?" Debbie asked.

"I'll talk to the judge in the morning," Patricia said. "I'll file a motion to dismiss the lawsuit. That won't stop them from bothering Sam about it, but at least it means they should leave you alone."

"Poor Sam." Janet shook her head.

"I'll go talk to him," Patricia said. "We won't let these Hollywood types push us around."

Janet wasn't sure what to expect when they opened the café Monday morning. Would the studio's lawyers be back? Would someone else threaten her with a lawsuit today?

She gazed over at the coffeepot. She'd already had two cups but was considering a third. She'd been so keyed up last night she knew she wouldn't be able to sleep, so she spent a couple hours working on the recipe book again, and then she'd gone ahead and ordered a copy. She'd see how it looked; she could always print more copies if it turned out well and seemed like the kind of thing people would want. For now, she just hoped it was the kind of thing Debbie would want.

Around lunchtime, Greg walked into the café wearing jeans and work boots, a leather bag slung over his shoulder. Janet saw several papers sticking out from under the flap.

"Hi, Greg," Janet called from behind the register.

"Fancy seeing you here," Paulette said, sidling up to her son.

Greg leaned in and gave her a hug. "It's good to see you."

"Hi," Debbie said, tucking her order notepad in her pocket. "What's up?"

"I wanted to talk to you both."

Janet looked around. There were a few occupied tables, but it was pretty slow today. The table in the corner had already paid their check and were just chatting, and the one by the register was finishing up their sandwiches.

"I can handle the tables," Paulette said.

Janet indicated a table in a quiet corner of the café, and Greg set his bag down on one of the chairs and opened it. "I went to the Department of Buildings first thing this morning," Greg said, as he pulled a folded oversized set of papers out. "It took some digging, but I found the set of plans that was filed with the city before Sunshine Cinemas was renovated in the forties." He unfolded the paper and spread it out on the table in front of them. Janet saw that they were architectural plans—she would have called them blueprints, but the paper was white instead of blue. "I actually found all kinds of interesting things in the file for the building. Some of the renovations that were done in later years were done without permits, it seems, which is interesting."

"So some of the renovations weren't legal?" Janet asked.

"Apparently not," Greg said. "But that's not all that unusual in a building that old."

"But what did you find out about the forties renovation?" Debbie asked. She leaned forward and squinted down at the pages on the table.

Greg laughed. "Okay, I'll cut to the chase. It seems the plans for the renovation were filed in January of 1944." He tapped the right corner of the pages, where the name of the architect and date were recorded. Janet made out what looked like a drawing of the theater with two auditoriums. "An architect named J.A. Wilson filed the plans, and a contractor named Heinrich Wilson, who I think was his son, did the actual work. The finished theater was inspected and the permits closed in November of 1944."

"It was 1944," Debbie repeated. "So Sam had the timeline wrong."

"Which means *we* had the timeline wrong. There weren't two years between the theft and when the film was hidden in the wall. The film was probably hidden in that wall shortly after it was stolen."

"And the theater was being renovated while Gable was in Dennison in 1944," Debbie said. "And we know he was for sure at the theater."

"Wait. Are you saying you think Gable could have hidden the film himself after all?" Janet looked from Debbie to Greg and back again.

"We don't know," Debbie said. "Not yet, I don't think. We still don't know why he would do that. He'd spent nearly two weeks and plenty of money on the project. Why would he just get rid of it?"

"And if he had wanted to get rid of it, why not just throw it away, or shred it, or something?" Greg asked. "Why bury it in the wall of the theater?"

"And even if he did bury it in the wall, why would he then report the film as stolen?" Janet added.

"It's hard to say, but we have to consider Clark a real possibility," Debbie said. "But also, this timing means that Frederick Hallman could have been behind it too. Or Bernie or May, for that matter."

"True," Janet said. "This doesn't help us eliminate any suspects. It just means we have one more suspect to consider."

"But we still don't know what really happened."

"Okay, let's think," Janet said. "What do we know?"

Debbie looked down at the oversized paper on the table. "This is the plan for the theater after the renovation, right?"

Greg nodded. "The before plans are underneath that."

Debbie lifted the top sheet off and gazed at the paper underneath. Janet studied it too. This page showed the footprint of the theater with one larger auditorium. There were more seats, and they were more spread out, according to the drawing.

"It seems that to be able to keep the theater open during the renovation, they removed all the seats, built the wall down the middle, and then got one side up and running as quickly as they could. So this side"—he pointed at the left auditorium—"was operating for most of the summer and fall of that year, while they didn't get the second screen working until later in the year."

"So September of 1944, they would have been showing a movie over here?" Janet pointed left of the line that divided the theater into two auditoriums.

"That's right," Greg said.

"And the film was found where?" Janet traced her finger along the line that represented the back of the theaters. "Here?"

"Right about there." Greg tapped the rear wall, on the right side. "It would have been in the part of the auditorium that wasn't functional yet."

"So someone took the film into the unfinished auditorium, looked around...and then what? How would it have gotten in the wall, even then?"

Greg blew out a breath. "My best guess is that the drywall was partially installed on that side. So the far side of the wall—the plaster and lath side—"

"The one backing the concession stand?" Janet said.

"Right," Greg said. "That side of the wall was untouched, but my guess is someone had started nailing up drywall on the renovation side. Maybe they'd installed drywall halfway up before leaving for the day."

Debbie nodded. "In which case, there would have been a space between the two sides of the wall where someone could have slipped the film canisters."

"They would have fallen to the floor, but if the bottom part of the wall was covered by drywall, they wouldn't be easily seen," Janet said.

"They would have been nearly invisible, unless someone knew to look for them between the studs," Greg said. "It's plausible."

"It's got to be what happened," Janet said. "How else would the film have gotten there?"

"But who put it there?" Debbie asked.

"That is the million-dollar question," Greg said.

Janet leaned in, pressing her elbows down on the table, trying to make sense of the black and white lines. "Are these the restrooms?" she asked, pointing to a couple of squares on one side of the lobby.

"That's right," Greg said. "Men's was over here, and this was the ladies'."

Janet tried to picture it. "Gayle said she was waiting for her friend Millie, who had gone to the restroom." She pointed to the ladies' restroom, which was on the side of the theater still under construction. "She said she was in the hallway by the popcorn machine, which means she was about here." She pointed to a spot on the plan to the right of the concession stand. "So if she saw Clark coming down the hallway, he had to have been coming from the area under renovation, right?"

"I think you're right." Debbie nodded. "Based on what Gayle told us, that has to be it."

"Was there anything else over this way?" Janet pointed to the short hallway.

"Just the emergency exit, there at the end."

"In that case"—Janet looked up at Debbie—"what was Clark Gable doing in a hallway that led to the theater that was under construction—"

"The very same theater where the film was found seventy years later—"

"—on the night the film went missing?" Janet finished.

"Huh."

"Huh is right." There were still plenty of things that didn't add up yet. It didn't all make sense—not yet. But if they were right…

Janet's eyes met Debbie's. She was thinking the exact same thing Janet was.

"It looks like we have a new lead suspect," Debbie said. "Now we just need to figure out why he would get rid of the film and then lie and say it was stolen."

CHAPTER NINETEEN

*A*fter they closed up, Janet headed home, but she kept thinking about the revelation of that afternoon. Had Clark Gable really been the one to leave the film in the half-built wall at the theater? If it was true, there had to be an explanation. What was she missing? She'd been through so many accounts and pieces of information. How did it all fit together?

Plus, how would the news, if it was true, affect the fight for ownership over the film? If the film had been stolen from Gable's hotel room, the estate had a pretty solid claim on it, or maybe the studio. But if Clark himself had abandoned the film, dumping it at the theater? Wouldn't that make a strong case for Sam being the rightful owner?

For now, though, she looked over her notes, trying to make sense of it all. Frederick the studio executive claimed to have seen Bernie by the door to Clark's room the night the film was stolen. There was no mention of the time. May admitted she had gone inside and noticed the film was gone around seven thirty. Gayle said Clark had visited her mother the day of the theft and asked her not to tell the police or anyone else about it. Helen's diary showed her disappointment over not spending time with Clark the night of the theft, or the night before.

Helen had recorded that Clark hadn't seemed like himself, that he wasn't so charming or flirty, when he came to the diner. That would have been later on the same day he'd gone to visit Dolores Zink. Did his meeting with Dolores affect his mood? Or was something else entirely going on?

Janet was getting frustrated. She wasn't getting anywhere new. She was about to pack it all in and start dinner when her phone rang. Debbie.

"Janet?" Her best friend's excitement came through in her voice. "They found more film."

"What?"

"Greg just called me to say that he was working in the basement of the theater this afternoon, and when he knocked down a wall, another film canister fell out. It matches the others."

"What?" Janet repeated as other words failed her. "For real?"

"Yes. We're headed over to the museum now. Kim is going to unlock it so we can use the projector. Can you come?"

"You're going to want to see this," Greg said from Debbie's end of the line.

Janet was already walking toward the door. "I'm on my way."

By the time Janet arrived at the Depot Museum, Kim had already set up the antique movie projector and threaded the new film into it. A silver canister, nearly identical to the ones they'd found before, sat on a table at the side of the room. Greg and Sam were there, as was Debbie.

"*Where* did you find this?" Janet asked, picking up the canister. It was labeled #3, *Addie.*

"It's the craziest thing," Greg said. "While I was working in the auditorium, framing in the new walls, I blew a fuse."

"That's not the crazy part," Sam said. "The wiring in that building is too old. It can't handle all these modern power tools."

"So I went down to the basement, where the fuse box is. It's in the load-bearing wall just under the concession stand."

"Which, as you probably remember, is just under the place where the other film was found," Sam added.

"For whatever reason, the stained plaster caught my eye this time," Greg said. "I've been down there a lot since I've been working on the theater, but this time, there was a chunk of drywall that just looked like it needed to come off. It was warped and stained and moldy, and I couldn't take it being there any longer."

"It all has to come off anyway to rewire the place," Sam said. "That was always the plan, but we were starting with the main level."

"But something about it was bothering me, so I just started pulling the drywall down," Greg continued. "It was so rotten it just crumbled in my hands. As I yanked a big chunk off, this came tumbling out and crashed right onto the floor."

"Best we can tell, it must have been dumped with the first two canisters but ended up falling," Sam said. "A part of the floorboard under the hiding place had rotted away, just enough that there was space for this canister to fall into the crevice between the drywall and the plaster and lath wall in the basement."

"So there were three film canisters there the whole time?" Janet asked, trying to make sense of this news.

"Maybe more. We don't know for sure," Sam said, his eyes wide. "Maybe we should just tear down all the walls to see what's in there."

"I don't know that we need to go that far," Greg said with a laugh. "But let's see what's on this one."

"I think I have it ready to go," Kim said.

Janet held her breath as Debbie shut off the lights. Would there be more interviews with folks in town? Maybe some interaction with one of the suspects that would give some insight into what had happened—Frederick Hallman confessing, maybe? Wait. No, that timing didn't make any sense at all. Well, maybe some interaction with Frederick that would tell them more, or—

Kim flipped the projector's switch and an image flashed onto the white wall. It was black and white, just like the other film strips, and grainy, but Janet could see that the image that appeared on the screen wasn't any place in Dennison. She knew exactly where it was, though.

"That's the house where Clark was born," Debbie said.

Janet nodded. It was the same two-story white house where the Clark Gable Birthplace and Museum now stood, except that in this shot, the house was run-down, the porch sagging, and the gutter leaning. Paint peeled off the siding, several of the windows were broken, and a section of the roof had started to cave in.

"It looks like it's in pretty bad shape," Greg said. The camera didn't move, just recorded the state of the house from the front. The only sound was some wind whipping around the camera.

"The house was torn down in the 1960s," Janet said. "What's there now is a reconstruction."

"Appears it had been empty for some time before it was pulled apart," Sam said. It was a bleak scene, made even more so by the absence of commentary. Then the scene cut off, and the next shot showed what must have been the interior of the same house. A wall with a fireplace stood at the far side, where the cash register was now in the modern reconstruction, and a couple of armchairs sat beside it. Everything appeared to be covered in a thick layer of dust, and cobwebs choked the corners of the room.

"I don't remember this room," said a voice that was undoubtedly Clark Gable's. "But it's almost as if I can feel it in my bones anyway. Something in me knows I've been here before." He turned the camera and panned around the room, revealing a sagging couch and a partially collapsed table. At some point, someone had scrawled graffiti on the front wall. They waited, but Clark didn't say anything more. The scene continued on silently.

"How old was he when his family moved out of this house?" Janet asked.

"Less than a year," Debbie said. "His mom was sick. Addie."

"Sick how?" Greg asked.

"It's not totally clear," Debbie said. "The doctors thought it might have been epilepsy, though some now think it was a progressive brain tumor. But as she got sicker, well, she was incapable of caring for him, and they left this house to move closer to her family."

"That's a bad situation," Sam said.

Debbie nodded. "It wasn't just the health problems, though. She was—it seems she was mentally ill, or maybe it was the brain tumor changing her behavior. Whatever it was, it sounds like she wasn't herself, or in her right mind, toward the end."

"How awful," Kim said quietly.

The shot cut off, and then the image of a gravestone appeared on the screen. *Addie Hershelman Gable, 1869-1901*, read the headstone in a bleak cemetery. Again, there was no sound except the wind.

"She actually died in 1900," Debbie said. "I read in his biography that her headstone had a mistake on it."

"How does that happen?" Janet asked.

Debbie shrugged.

"This film is very different," Kim said, echoing the thought that had been in Janet's head as well.

"It's strange," Debbie said, and it looked like she was going to say more, but then the scene changed, and a woman was on the screen, her curly dark hair, threaded with white, framing her face. She wore a long-sleeved floral dress and sat on a divan of some sort.

"Please state your name," Gable said.

"Marie Fassbender," she said. "William Gable—your father—was my uncle."

"You met my mother, Addie?" Gable asked.

"Just a couple of times," Marie said. "I didn't go to their wedding. I don't know that anyone did, actually. But I met her at Christmas one year, probably when I was, oh, eight or so. You weren't born yet, I don't think."

"What do you remember about her?" Clark asked.

"She was quiet," Marie said. "She was kind to me, I do remember that. But she seemed uncomfortable."

"How so?"

"Oh, I don't know. I just remember thinking that my parents were right, and she didn't really fit in."

"Your parents thought she didn't fit in?"

"She was… she was just different, I guess."

"What do you mean?"

Marie shifted in her seat. She pulled at the edge of her sleeve. She seemed to make some sort of decision, because the tone of her voice changed after that. "She was always very kind to me. That's all I know."

"Can you tell me more about what you mean, saying she was different?"

Marie smiled, just a little too brightly. "She was a caring mother, that's what everyone said. She loved you as best she could."

"What do you mean?" Clark said.

Marie tugged at her sleeve again, twisting the fabric between her fingers.

"Oh, Clark," she finally said. "You don't want to hear about all that."

"I do, though," he said. "That's why I'm here. That's the whole reason I'm in this town. To learn about her. Please, tell me what you know."

Marie took in a long breath and blew it out slowly. Then, she said, "I don't know. I was only a kid at the time. I'm afraid I really can't tell you anything about it."

After that, the scene ended, and the screen went black. Janet looked over at Debbie, who met her gaze, her eyes wide. Clark had just admitted that the real reason he was in Dennison wasn't to make the film, it was to learn more about his mother. If that was true—and Janet didn't know why he would lie to his cousin—it changed everything.

In the scene that came next, the camera appeared to be mounted or placed in the passenger seat of a car, recording the flat Ohio countryside as it went by.

"So, was the story about making the documentary ever true?" Debbie asked.

"I think it must have been," Janet said, thinking aloud. "He did all those interviews. He spent nearly two weeks in Dennison. He wouldn't have done all that if he just needed a cover story, right?"

"Film was expensive enough back then that it does seem unlikely," Greg said.

"He'd just come off making that other documentary," Janet said. "It would make sense if he had intended to make this other one. But maybe it explains why he chose Dennison, of all places, to make the film. Perhaps the film was real but he had an ulterior motive in coming here."

"To learn more about the mother he never knew," Debbie said.

Janet looked back at the screen as the image changed again.

She sucked in a breath.

"Oh my. Is that—"

"I think it must be," Debbie said, just before the woman on the screen started talking, and they knew for sure that they were looking at Dolores Zink.

CHAPTER TWENTY

Dennison, Ohio
September 27, 1944

Clark finished setting up the camera and turned to
Dolores.

"I don't think I want to be filmed," Dolores said.

"You look very nice," Clark said. She did. She was
a very handsome woman, tall and regal. She was
seated on a tufted settee with a carved wooden frame,
and the walls behind her were covered in a soft floral
wallpaper. She called this room the good parlor, and
he could see why.

"I don't want to be in any movie."

"I promise you, I'm not planning to use this footage in my film."

"Then why record it at all?" Dolores asked.

"So I can look back at this, in case I miss any-thing." There was a pause, while Dolores adjusted a pillow next to her. *"I won't show it to anyone."*

He waited while Dolores considered this. *"I don't know that you're going to want to revisit what I have to tell you, unfortunately,"* Dolores said. *"But I told your mother I would always look out for you and help you.... Do you promise you won't put this in a movie? I wouldn't want people to think I was..."*

She struggled to find the word she was looking for. Clark had to bite his tongue to not offer suggestions. Better to just let her talk.

"My husband doesn't approve of moving pictures. Or movie stars, truth be told."

Clark laughed. *"He's right to be wary. Many of us are scoundrels. But I promise. And I'm grateful you're willing to talk to me."*

"Well, all right. Like I said, I promised your mother," Dolores said. *"What do you want to know?"*

"Everything," Clark said.

"What do you already know?"

Clark took a deep breath. *"My father always told me that my mother died when I was a baby because she was sick. I knew she had epilepsy, so I guess I didn't ask too many questions. But Carole—that was my wife—she always thought it was strange I didn't know much about her, and that my family never talked about her. It wasn't as if I saw my family much anyway, but still, Carole always thought there was something more going on. Things were so busy with the studio, and with the war going on, I didn't think about it too much, but after Carole—"*

He broke off. It was still hard even to think about, let alone say aloud.

"It was tragic, what happened," Dolores said.

Clark felt tears sting his eyes, and he bit them back. He couldn't cry. Not now. Not here.

"After Carole passed, and I joined up, I started thinking about it more. I had a lot of time to think, overseas, and I guess I just... It seemed like it was finally time to see if I could learn more about her, so here I am. There aren't too many people left around here who remember her." Clark stifled a sniffle. "How did you know my mother?"

"I was born in Cadiz, same as you were," Dolores said. "We had a farm. My brothers helped out with the farm. We never had a lot, but things were fine until the summer of 1900, when the crops failed. It didn't rain hardly at all that whole summer, and everything just dried up and died. I was thirteen, and I remember thinking we were going to be homeless. My parents

very nearly did lose the farm, but Dad managed to bor-
row enough from Mama's family to hold on to it. Well,
anyway, things were very tight, and Mama had just
had Gideon, so she couldn't go out looking for a job, so
I got work cooking and cleaning for different families
in town. One of those was your family."

"My mother hired you to cook and clean?"

"It was actually your father who hired me," Dolores
said. "Your mother was—well, he said her health was
delicate, but I quickly realized that wasn't all."

"What do you mean?" This was it. This was what
no one ever talked about.

"Your mother was six months along or so by that
point, and she needed to rest a lot," Dolores said. "But
also, she would go into these rages sometimes. I don't
know what they were really. I called them her spells.
But she would yell and sometimes throw things, and it
was like she didn't even know what she was doing. I
would try my best to settle her down, and then it would
pass, and she would be back to her usual self."

"She would yell and throw things?"

"When she was lucid, she was the sweetest thing.
It wasn't like her at all, which is what made it so fright-
ening when it did happen."

"Why did she do that?"

"I couldn't say," Dolores said. "I once heard that she was being treated with hydrotherapy. I didn't know what it was at the time, but now I know it's for, well, people who have a mental sickness of some kind. It seems something wasn't right in her brain. But at the time, I was just a kid, and I didn't understand much except that she needed help cooking and cleaning and, occasionally, settling down."

"My mother had a mental illness."

"I don't know that for sure. I suspected, but no one ever said that to me."

"But you think so."

"I..." Dolores was struggling to figure out how to respond. "They never told you?" she finally asked.

"No."

"I'm sorry."

"Thank you for being honest with me. You're the first one who ever has been."

"It was a different time. I know your father did the best he could. And it just got harder for them after you were born. I don't mean to say—in some ways, it was much better. She doted on you. She wouldn't let you out of her sight. No matter what else, please know that she loved you fiercely. But it was hard for her. She wasn't getting enough sleep, and so the episodes came more regularly, and—well, I think we were all struggling, *trying to figure out what to do. Eventually, it got to be too much, and in the fall, they went to be closer to your mother's family."*

Clark didn't know what to say. After a minute of silence, Dolores continued.

"She loved you, you know. Even when she was— well, her thoughts were always about her baby boy."

"How long did you work for my mother?"

"I was there until they moved. I was so sad to see them go. I was there most days by that point and had come to love you as my own. And I'd become quite close to your mother by that point as well."

"Did she want to go?"

"I think she knew they didn't have a choice," Dolores said. "She was struggling. Even she knew it." Dolores dabbed at her eyes with a tissue. "I think she was afraid, to be honest. She didn't know what was going to happen, only that she couldn't control the episodes. She asked me to promise her that I would always look out for you."

"How would you have done so, if she'd moved away?"

"I don't know what she was thinking," Dolores said. "I don't know if she did either. But I agreed, of course. And I've done my best. I sent letters for a while, but finally your father wrote back and told me she'd passed. I mourned for her, I truly did. I knew you were being raised by your family at that point, but I always followed your career."

There was a beat of silence, and then Dolores added, "She loved you more than anything."

"Thank you for saying that." It felt good to hear it.

"It's true. I know this is probably not what you were hoping to hear, but it's true."

"I wanted to hear the truth. I thank you for giving it to me. My father's family never did."

"They were trying to protect you."

"They did the best they could."

There was another beat of silence. The ticking of a clock echoed loudly in the silent room.

"What will you do, now that you know?"

"I don't know," Clark said. He needed time to think. It would take a while to absorb all of this. But then, a moment later, he added, "But this changes things."

The screen went black.

"Oh my." Debbie's eyes were wide.

"That's a terrible story," Kim said. "How awful, to learn that about your mother."

They were right, of course. It was a terrible thing to have to hear. Janet could understand why the family had protected Clark from this knowledge. But also, her mind was spinning, thinking through the timeline.

"According to Gayle Zink, who was a child at the time, this interview happened the same day the film disappeared," Janet said.

"I believe so," Debbie said. "Then, according to Helen Fletcher's diaries, he was weird that night at the diner, and said filming hadn't gone well."

"He'd come to Dennison to find out about his mother," Janet said, picking up the thread. "After this interview, he was no doubt busy absorbing the terrible news he'd learned."

"And then, that night the film disappeared," Debbie said.

Janet nodded. It all fit together.

"I noticed you both said 'disappeared,' not 'was stolen,'" Greg said.

"I guess we did," Debbie said. "Probably because we don't actually think it was stolen, not anymore."

"Helen Fletcher may have tried to take it, but I suspect she wasn't successful, either because she wasn't able to get into the room or because the film canisters were already gone when she did," Janet said.

"Frederick Hallman probably would have stolen them if he could have, but he didn't," Debbie said. "Bernard insisted he didn't do it. May was never really in consideration."

"Once Clark had learned the truth, he didn't want to stick around and finish the film," Janet said. "So he scrapped the project, tossed the film he'd shot where he thought no one would ever find it, and left town."

"But why would he scrap the whole thing?" Kim asked. "If he'd been working on it for two weeks, that was a lot of money and time down the drain."

"Maybe his heart wasn't in it anymore," Janet said. "All along we were wondering why he didn't just reshoot the scenes. Now we know why. He didn't want to, because he'd learned what he'd come to find out."

"Maybe the whole thing was a cover story the whole time. Maybe he never intended to make the film at all, but it was just an excuse to be here while he tried to find out the truth," Debbie added.

"Whatever was going on, I think this interview changed things. He even said so himself," Janet said. "And he abandoned it all and hatched a plan to get rid of the film."

"But what about the robbery?" Sam said. "Why report it stolen? Why not just quietly abandon the project? By reporting it stolen, he wasted so many people's time and put several reputations on the line. It became a national news story. Why would he do that?"

With his words, something else clicked into place. "Because it would create a national news story," Janet said slowly. "What's that they say? All publicity is good publicity?"

"Frederick Hallman," Debbie said, nodding. "That's it. That's what he was getting at. He didn't steal the film, but he did figure out a way to get Clark back to Los Angeles, and get publicity for Gable to boot."

"You think it was Hallman's idea to report the film as stolen, knowing it wasn't?" Greg asked. "For publicity?"

"If he did, it worked," Janet said. "Clark reported the theft, and it became headline news, just like he knew it would, and suddenly the biggest star was back in the headlines and back in Hollywood."

"Exactly. A savvy studio executive could have seen the opportunity in this. We know Hallman was savvy," Debbie said. "And we also know he got a big promotion shortly afterward."

"But why would Clark go along with it?" Kim asked. "If we're right, even if he didn't engineer the whole theft story, he lied to the police."

"Maybe he didn't see it that way," Janet said, shaking her head. "I mean, we can't possibly know for sure, but he was an actor. An academy-award winning one at that. Maybe he saw it as playing a role."

"The role of the aggrieved theft victim?" Greg asked.

"It's a good theory," Debbie said.

"We may never know for sure if that's how it went down," Janet said. "But it's the most plausible scenario I've heard so far."

"And it would explain why the police never found out what happened to the film," Debbie added. "They never considered that Clark could have stolen the film himself. That it could all be an elaborate ruse."

It wasn't proof, but it felt right to Janet. Given everything they'd learned, and all the pieces that had come together, it felt to her like this had to be the right answer.

"Huh." Greg was nodding. "It makes sense, in a way."

"It does." Kim was slowly unwinding the film and rolling it back up. "I wonder if there are any more canisters of film in that theater?"

"If there are, we'll find them," Greg promised.

"In the meantime, make sure to keep this safe," Debbie said, nodding to the film. Kim was now snapping the lid back on the canister.

"The bank's closed for today," Sam said. "But I'll lock this up in the office for tonight and secure it with the others first thing in the morning."

Janet felt like she should offer the safe at the café, but the memory of being served papers over possession of the film was too fresh. This roll of film would be fine in the theater for one night.

When they walked out of the museum a few minutes later, Janet was even more convinced they'd figured it out. She was so sure of it that she almost didn't see the man in the car, watching them.

"Do you see that guy?" Debbie asked, elbowing her. "In the black car?"

Janet looked over and saw the same black Ford she'd seen before in the parking lot.

"I've seen him before," Debbie said.

"Me too." Janet suddenly felt a thread of fear working its way up her spine.

"Do you think he's following us?"

"I think that's a fair assumption, at this point," Janet said.

"Do you think we should let Ian know?"

"Yes," Janet said. "I think we probably should."

CHAPTER TWENTY-ONE

By the time Ian arrived at the parking lot outside the museum, the man in the car was gone. He'd left shortly after Greg and Sam left, and though Janet had tried to record the license plate number, she hadn't managed to get more than the first two numbers. Ian recorded them and then listened to their descriptions of the times they'd seen the man in the car around town.

"Why didn't you tell me before this?" Ian asked, shaking his head.

"I guess I wasn't sure," Janet said.

"If you see anything more suspicious, either of you, please let me know," Ian said. He and Janet followed Debbie as she drove home and made sure she got in safely before they went home together.

They had a quiet dinner. She updated him on all they'd learned that day, and then they got ready for bed. Janet got a notification that the cookbook would arrive the next day. She couldn't wait to see it. Her mind wouldn't stop spinning, but she was exhausted, and she gratefully climbed under the covers that night.

Janet was just about to turn off the light when Ian's phone buzzed. He reached for where it was plugged into the charger on the nightstand. Janet hesitated, her hand hovering inches from the light, as he read a message.

"It's the theater," Ian said. "I have to go."

"What do you mean, it's the theater?" Janet sat up in bed, but Ian was already pulling on his clothes.

"Someone broke into the theater. Vaughn thinks they're still there." Ian rushed out of the room and for the stairs. Janet threw a sweater on over her pajama top and rushed after him. Ian was already headed for the door, keys in hand. "I don't know how long I'll be gone. You might as well go to bed."

"Not a chance. I'm coming with you. The film is at the theater." Janet grabbed her phone, her keys, and her jacket and followed Ian out the door. Janet didn't know if he truly didn't care or just didn't have the time to argue, but he didn't fight her when she climbed into his police cruiser and buckled herself into the passenger seat.

"I thought the film was in a lock box at the bank?" Ian said as he backed the car out of the driveway.

"The first two rolls are, but the new one discovered today is at the theater, because the bank was closed." Janet held on to the door handle as Ian pressed on the gas pedal and raced down the street. "It was another roll of the Clark Gable footage. We watched it at the museum."

"I thought there wasn't a safe at the theater?"

"I don't think there is. But he wasn't going to ask us to hold on to it, so what was he going to do? He said he would lock it in the office and it would be okay for the night."

"Who knew it was at the theater?"

"Just me and Debbie, Greg, Kim, and Sam," Janet said. They turned right, toward the downtown area. A few of the houses had lights on, but most were dark as they zoomed past. "Though—oh, Ian. What about that man in the car?"

"Is there any chance he followed Sam tonight?"

"Maybe," Janet said. "He left not long after they all did. Do you think he was following Sam too?"

"I think we should assume the answer to that is yes," Ian said.

He didn't say anything more before he pulled up outside the theater. "Stay here," he barked, and then ran to meet two uniformed police officers in front, both on high alert. In the gloom of the moonless night, Janet couldn't tell who they were, but she assumed one of them was Vaughn. She could see that the glass door had been shattered and the doorway gaped open. After a quick conference with the man, Ian put his hand on the holster at his hip—when had he grabbed that?—and walked inside.

Janet said a prayer for his safety and for the safety of all the officers here tonight. She knew Ian wasn't wearing his bulletproof vest, and every time he answered a call there was a chance he was putting his life on the line. She'd been married to a police officer long enough to know that he would do whatever it took to keep his town safe, but she was so rarely there to watch him walk into danger. She prayed with everything she had that he would be all right.

A minute passed, and then two, and Janet tried to breathe. What was happening inside the theater?

Then, someone walked out the door. His hands were in his pockets, and he was hurrying away from the theater. It wasn't Ian, and it wasn't an officer in uniform. Was it—

But when the man walked away from the theater and into the light of a streetlamp, she recognized him. She pushed open the car door.

"Sam!"

Sam turned his head. Janet stepped out of the car and waved. "What's going on?" she called.

Sam hurried to Janet, and he was breathing hard and sweating when he came up next to her.

"Someone's inside," he said.

"Still?"

He nodded. "I was sitting at home and just had a bad feeling about that film being left here. I checked in on the security system, just to make sure things were okay, and found the system was down. So I came down here, and when I arrived I saw that the door had been smashed in."

"What do you mean the system was down?"

"Totally offline. Wirelessly jammed, I'm sure. I should have known these guys were serious. I called the police, but then I went in and he was still there. I saw a blur of a man in black clothing heading toward the lobby."

"You didn't follow him, did you?"

"Of course I did. He went down the hallway, to the door to the left auditorium, but then he vanished. By that time the police were here—they don't mess around in this town, thank goodness—and they had the building surrounded, and didn't see him come out. They think he's still inside somewhere. I tried to find him, but I don't know where he is. When Ian arrived, he told me in no uncertain terms to vacate the premises, so here I am."

"So the thief is hiding in the theater somewhere?"

"That's what we think."

"And did he get the film?"

"Yes. On my way out the door, I checked the office, and it's gone."

"I really hope they find him." Janet kept her eyes trained on the theater door, watching for movement. "Did you see who it was?"

"It's got to be the same guy who was following me," Sam said. "Some goon hired by the Hollywood studio, I'm betting."

"So he was following you too?" Janet said. Of course he had been. How silly she and Debbie had been to think they were the only ones being observed. If the man was trying to get his hands on the film, he would be watching all of them. "Where could he be now?" Janet asked, even though she knew it was pointless to ask. If Sam knew, they wouldn't be here.

"I don't know."

Janet pictured the inside of the theater in her mind. She saw the plastic sheeting, ghostly in the dim light. The partially framed walls, and the walls that had been mostly torn down. The dark hallways and shadowy corners. The decrepit bathrooms with their dank stalls. The whole basement, which Janet hadn't even seen. There were so many places to hide.

She heard a squawk on the officer's radio. Vaughn walked toward the corner and looked around, then went back to his post by the front door. She prayed, once again, for Ian's safety, and marveled at how brave her husband was.

Sam paced as they waited. Janet suspected he felt as helpless as she did. But as they waited, she turned the unfolding events over in her mind. Something didn't make sense.

"What is the point of stealing the film?" she asked. "Assuming the thief has been hired by the studio, what's he going to do with it?"

"Use it to make money," Sam said. "Even if there's not enough there to make a film out of, they could sell it to a tabloid or something. Someone would pay for that footage."

"But once it was reported stolen, anyone who sold it would be pretty easy to track down as the thief."

"Maybe," Sam said. "I mean, sure, it would be hard for a studio to release a feature film made from stolen footage. But someone could put it up online and rack up views and make money on ads. If they were smart, it would be hard to trace. The police might eventually track down who originated the videos, but not before they'd made a fair amount in ad revenue."

Janet realized he was probably right. The internet offered plenty of ways to make money if you didn't care about ethics. Someone could hide behind screen names and shell companies and make themselves very difficult to track down. Whoever held that film was sitting on a potential gold mine, even if the footage they held was stolen. The police would probably find them eventually, but they could cash in in the meantime. For some, it might seem like a gamble worth taking.

There was a thunderous crash from somewhere inside the theater. Janet let out a little yelp. Was Ian okay? Another squawk from his radio, and then Vaughn walked to the left, away from the corner. What was going on in there?

Janet held her breath as she waited. The night was gloomy and dark, with a bitter wind that whipped through the streets. Away from the streetlight, it was so dark that at first she almost didn't see it. A movement over at the corner of the building.

"What's that?" she said. If it was the thief, he'd snuck out a side door. But the police had the place surrounded, didn't they? How would he have gotten out?

Sam's head whipped around to where she was pointing. Then he yelled. "Hey! Over there!"

Vaughn started running back past the theater, and the man—she was pretty sure now that it was a man—took off running, sprinting down Spring Street. He must have gotten out through a side door. But how had the officers inside let him go? It took everything in her not to rush into the theater to see if Ian was okay. She watched as the man ran along Spring Street, Vaughn on his tail.

And then, from the next block, someone sprinted toward him. Ian. How had he gotten there? Janet didn't understand what was happening, but she saw the moment the thief realized he was caught, Vaughn behind him and Ian coming at him. He froze, and then tried to pivot to the right to race across the street, but Vaughn got there first. He tackled the man, and as he fell, something round flew out from under his coat and landed with a crash on the pavement. The film canister! A moment later Ian slapped handcuffs on him, and Vaughn collected the canister.

"Got him," Sam said, pumping his fist. Janet let out a pent-up breath.

Janet wanted to run over and throw her arms around Ian, but she knew enough to stay out of the way. She watched as the other officers came out of the theater and Ian read the thief his rights and escorted him to Vaughn's squad car.

Ian came over to Janet and Sam, the film canister in a plastic bag in his hands.

"We'll have to take this in for evidence, I'm afraid."

"That's quite all right. Better to have it at the police station for now," Sam said. "Thank you for coming so quickly, and for stopping him."

Ian smiled. "That's kind of our thing. That's what we do." He turned to Janet. "It's going to be a long night. You'd probably better head on home."

Janet wanted to protest—she had so many questions about what had happened inside that theater—but the truth was, she was exhausted. Ian was safe now, and the film was in good hands, and she knew Ian would explain later. "I'll meet you at home."

CHAPTER TWENTY-TWO

Ⅰt wasn't until the next afternoon that Janet had the chance to talk to Ian to find out what had happened inside the theater. Janet filled Debbie in on what she did know as soon as she came into the café the next morning.

"He stole the film from the theater? Why would he do that?" Debbie interjected, and Janet explained the theory Sam had floated. "I'm so glad they caught him."

"Me too," Janet said. "But Ian got in very late, and he was sound asleep when I got up this morning, so I don't know what they got out of the thief. I texted him to ask him to let us know when he gets a chance."

A few of their new regulars were still hanging around, including Evan and Seth and Annie and Ravi. Janet wondered if any of them knew anything about the attempted robbery last night, but it wasn't her place to ask. Ian would be investigating, so she just smiled and welcomed them.

Ian texted back a while later and said he could come by the café around three to share what he knew. Janet and Debbie let Sam, Greg, Kim, and Patricia know, so they could hear the update as well. They were all as invested in this as Janet and Debbie were.

After they closed the café at two, Janet, Debbie, and Paulette cleaned up, volleying theories back and forth.

"It had to be one of the studios who hired the guy," Debbie said. "They weren't getting answers quickly enough, so one of them decided to take it."

"The studio that filed a lawsuit against us—would they go to such extreme means when they already had a legal case pending?" Janet asked.

"Filing a legal case was a pretty extreme measure in the first place," Debbie said.

"But as far as the studios knew, the film was locked up at the bank," Janet said.

"Except whoever was following Sam," Debbie said. "He must have figured out that more film was discovered and that it was stored at the theater for the night. He knew that was his chance, and went for it."

"But we're back to who, and why," Paulette said. "What were they going to do with it? If they used the footage, the police would be able to discover who stole it."

The amateur sleuths were going around in circles, and Janet was glad when the others started arriving shortly before three.

"So, what you're telling me is that the Clark Gable film was stolen *again*?" Kim said as she walked inside the café.

"Correct. But it was recovered much more quickly this time," Janet said with a laugh.

"Janet was the one who spotted the guy," Sam said. "She's the one who saw him first."

"I might have spotted him, but I did nothing even remotely close to stopping him. That was all the work of the police."

Sam explained to the others how he'd had a bad feeling and checked in on the theater via his wireless security system. When he'd seen that the whole system was offline, he'd suspected it was being jammed and had come down to the theater and caught the guy in the act.

"He must have been at least somewhat sophisticated to have access to equipment that could mess up your system like that," Paulette said.

"He would need a certain amount of knowledge, but it turns out the equipment to make that happen isn't that expensive or hard to come by," Sam said. "Which I know now."

"It's a good thing you thought to check," Kim said, and Sam nodded.

Ian strode into the café just after three.

"He was working for a celebrity gossip site," Ian said by way of introduction. "The site was hoping to put the film up online and rack up advertising dollars. He was just a hired man whose pay-check depended on getting access to the film."

"But they didn't even know what was *on* that roll of film," Janet said. "No one did, except for a few of us."

"And what was on that roll probably wouldn't have been a crowd-pleaser," Debbie added.

"I don't think it really mattered. They just know Clark Gable's missing film rolls had been found, and they wanted it."

"And it wasn't the film studio that filed the lawsuit, then," Patricia said. "Or the Gable estate."

"Not the film studio," Ian said. "Not any of the legitimate options for the outcome here."

"So Sam was right," Janet added.

"Naturally." Sam grinned and took a bow.

"We're working on tracking down the people who hired him, but in the meantime, the roll of film is safe," Ian said.

"That's good," Janet said. "Now we just need to figure out what to do with them."

"It will probably take a while to sort out the legal ownership of the film," Patricia said. "But if we can make a case that Gable got rid of the film himself, the estate's case will be weakened. It seems pretty clear to me the film now belongs to Sam, who can turn around and sell it to the highest bidder. But it will still take some time to get that sorted out in the courts."

"It's not going to the highest bidder," Sam said. "The last roll we saw, the one about Gable's mother…well, I'm not sure about that one. Seems to me the right thing to do might be to give that one to the estate in any case. To honor his wish that that not be made public."

"That would be a nice outcome," Janet said.

"But as for those rolls of film that feature people from town? Those belong to Dennison. Once we get the legal issues sorted out, I'm donating them to the museum. If you'll have them, that is."

Kim pressed her lips together and seemed to be fighting back tears. She took in a breath, let it out, and nodded. "That would be amazing," she said. "I was able to track down the family of Danny Maldanado, that young soldier who was from Dennison. He still has family in town. I'm sure it would mean a lot to them to be able to see it."

"That would be wonderful," Sam agreed.

"What's on those rolls of film is a part of this town's history," Kim said. "I agree that it should belong to the town. But—are you sure? There are a lot of film studios who would pay top dollar for it."

"It could be life-changing money," Greg added.

"I don't need my life to change. Now that I'm back in Dennison, I have everything I've ever wanted," Sam said. "It will go to the museum, as long as I can show it sometimes on the big screen once my theater opens."

"You can show it any time you want." Kim laughed and dabbed her eyes.

Janet hoped she would have the selflessness to do the same thing if she was in Sam's place, if the film had been found at the café instead of the theater. But it hadn't, and she was in awe of Sam's generosity and thoughtfulness. That film probably would have been found sooner or later, but she was glad it had been found by such a solid guy. Janet knew how lucky she was to live in this special town, but sometimes things like this happened and she was reminded all over again.

They all stayed and chatted for a few minutes longer, and then people started to drift off, Ian back to the office and Greg and Sam back to the theater. Janet and Debbie locked up.

"We solved another one," Debbie said with a grin.

"It's kind of funny how it keeps happening, isn't it?" Janet said.

"It turns out we make a great team," Debbie said.

They walked to their cars together, and then Janet drove home. She had big plans with a thick novel and a mug of hot cocoa, but when she got home, she found a package on her doorstep. The cookbook! She carried it inside and ripped open the packaging, and the book slid out.

Recipes from the Whistle Stop Café.

It was wonderful. She flipped through the pages, looking at the recipes themselves. It had turned out nicely. The paper was thick, the printing professional, and the book was beautiful.

Janet pulled it to her chest. She was excited to give it to her best friend. Sooner or later, Debbie and Greg would set a wedding date, and she would be ready.

She couldn't wait to see what happened next.

Dear Reader,

It was so much fun to dive into the golden age of film in this story, and to weave real history and imagination together to create this book. I have to admit I am not a huge film buff, and I haven't seen most of the films from the forties and fifties, but when the editors of this series asked if I wanted to create a story around a lost film from one of the famous American actors who also fought in World War II, I knew this could be a fun story, and I jumped at the chance.

Much of the information about Clark Gable's life in this book is true—he was born William Clark Gable in Cadiz, Ohio, and his mother had him secretly baptized at the Catholic church in Dennison. His mother did die when he was very young, and she suffered from some mysterious ailment that apparently made her last days challenging. Gable's father moved the family from Cadiz to be closer to family as her health and mental state worsened in her later days. Gable went on to have a successful career in film as an actor for MGM, and he did join the army after the death of his third wife, Carole Lombard, who was killed in a plane crash while selling war bonds. The film studio where he was under contract did not want their biggest star to be in danger, but Gable not only fought in five combat missions, he also made a film for the army called *Combat America*, a documentary about the 351st Bombardment Group of the US Army in England during World War II.

Warren G. Harris's *Clark Gable: A Biography* was a big help to me as I researched the star's life.

I tried to stick to the facts as much as I could, but of course much of this story is imagined. There is no evidence that Clark Gable ever went to Dennison to make a film, for instance, and the idea of the lost film rolls is fictional, at least to my knowledge. Most of the businesses mentioned in Dennison in this book from the forties are fictional, including (alas!) the theater. There was no shady studio executive, nor hotel manager. If Gable ever did abandon a film project, he didn't claim it was stolen for publicity.

But I like to think that if Gable had shown up in Ohio during the war, it might have gone something like this. During those dark days of the war, a visit from the biggest star in Hollywood—and a veteran, to boot—would probably have made the people of the town pretty excited. And if he *had* decided to make a movie about the war effort on the home front, he couldn't have picked a better town than Dennison, where the depot's volunteers went out of their way to make soldiers feel welcome and safe as they went off to or returned home from war.

I hope you enjoyed reading this story as much as I enjoyed writing it.

Best,
Beth Adams

ABOUT the AUTHOR

Beth Adams lives in Brooklyn, New York, with her husband and two young daughters. When she's not writing, she's trying to find time to read mysteries.

A GLIMPSE *of the* PAST

When Clark Gable joined the army in 1942, he was under contract with the film studio MGM, which meant that he wasn't technically allowed to join up. The studio worked with the US Army to find Gable a role—making a film—that would keep him relatively safe, though he did serve in combat. Gable's contract also meant that he wouldn't have been allowed to make his own independent film, as he does in this book. That particular project is entirely fictional.

Back in the 1930s and 1940s, actors and actresses were actually employees of the film studios they had signed with, and were often cast in whatever roles the studios wanted them to appear in. Clark Gable is reported to have signed a contract with MGM in 1931 for $350 a week, and he starred in eight movies for the company that year, as well as two more for Warner Brothers (he was "loaned out" by MGM for these roles). When actors became more successful, they sometimes had more sway and got more say in their roles, but the studios still owned their name, image, and voice.

Many of the most famous actors and actresses of the era, including Gable, Greta Garbo, Joan Crawford, Cary Grant, and Rock Hudson, were brought up through the studio system.

FROM the HOME-FRONT KITCHEN

Clark Gable's Summer Salmon Salad

This recipe comes from the August 1941 edition of the magazine *Modern Screen*, which profiles how Clark Gable and his third wife Carole Lombard liked to entertain in the summer. According to the article, "Informality's the rule at the Gable farm. Clark and Carole love to have company drift in around dinnertime and stay for a feed—providing they help prepare it themselves. And if it's a July night, hot and breathless, you'll find the Gables out beneath the stars. Supper is served picnic style on the porch." This Summer Salmon recipe is one the Gables loved to serve at these gatherings, according to the magazine. The recipe calls for vegetable or mineral oil, but I would use extra virgin olive oil today. No measurements are given for the spices at the end, so I would start with a pinch of each and adjust according to taste.

To serve four:

Ingredients:

1 small head lettuce

1 can salmon

1 onion, minced fine

2 tomatoes, quartered

2 green peppers

2 eggs, hard-boiled

1 tablespoon vinegar

2 tablespoons vegetable or
   mineral oil

1 teaspoon lemon juice

Salt, pepper, paprika, garlic salt,
   and celery salt

Directions:

1. Trim off chilled head lettuce, tear off crisp leaves, and arrange in bowl.

2. Open can of salmon and empty into a soup plate. Remove bones and pieces of skin. Add minced onions and heart of lettuce chopped fine.

3. Arrange salmon and onion on lettuce, garnish with quartered tomatoes, sliced hard-boiled eggs, and green peppers sliced in thin rings.

4. To fish oil remaining in soup plate add vegetable oil, lemon juice, vinegar, and seasoning—mix well and pour over salad. Keep salad in cool place until serving. (To enlarge for unexpected company, add cool, sliced boiled potatoes and diced radishes.)

Read on for a sneak peek of another exciting book
in the Whistle Stop Café Mysteries *series!*

APPLE BLOSSOM TIME

BY RUTH LOGAN HERNE

We need to do a complete reset on all three sides of the house if you want to regain control of these plots." Janet Shaw's regretful expression said more than her words as she studied the tangled gardens flanking Greg Connor's home. The cozy cape cod, tucked into the sloped side of the street, was surrounded by what had been pretty plots at one time. Debbie Albright knew that because the gardens in family photos looked nothing like this when her fiancé's boys were young.

The word *jungle* offered a more apt description on this first Tuesday of April. Debbie had asked her best friend and business partner to come by and offer advice. Greg's wife had passed away six years before, and he had been left to raise two sons, Jaxon and Julian, whose memories of their mother grew faint with time. Their mother had overseen these gardens with the same love she'd shown her family. Debbie was determined to get these borders back into shape.

Janet wasn't known for her green thumb, but the simple and tasteful landscaping around her home indicated she knew something about gardening. That was more than Debbie could say personally.

The combined effect of Janet's tone and expression didn't bode well. Clearly a reset wasn't something to be undertaken lightly.

Debbie mulled the mess at her feet. The higher angle of the sun had brought shoots to life. A lot of them. Way too many for the size of the plots. She shifted her attention back to Janet. "I have no idea what a total reset means, but it sounds like we're signing up for 'Extreme Makeover, Garden Edition.'"

Janet laughed. "Holly Connor used to call gardening her therapy, and she loved perennials. She appreciated how the house nestles into a mild slope, and established English country gardens all around the perimeter."

"If this is what gardens look like in the UK, I'm proud to be an American." Debbie made a face. "This isn't a garden. It's a thicket. There's like, twenty saplings over there." She pointed to several whip-like things sticking up from the ground. "Even a novice like me knows that can't be good."

Janet sighed. "The gardens were gorgeous through that final year, and even the year after she passed away. She had a knack for making it look unplanned, like the garden just happened along without anyone taking the time to plant it. Not everybody can do that. Then she was gone." Janet grimaced. "The perennials staged a coup, sending out roots and seeds and randomly popping up all over. Then the weeds took over."

"I recognize those." Debbie pointed to the tulips and daffodils. The daffodils were in full bloom, nodding bright yellow and ivory heads in the early April breeze. The tulips would follow soon after. Maybe in time for an Easter bouquet. That much she knew. "Everything else is a complete mystery."

"Fortunately, we're good at solving mysteries!"

Debbie smiled and drew a deep breath. "I'm in uncharted water here, and not just about the gardens."

Janet faced her, a puzzled look on her face. "About marrying Greg? And creating a family with him and the boys?"

"Not that, no." Debbie dissuaded that notion quickly. "Greg makes me ridiculously happy. And I love the boys. They're such good kids. Although they do manage to give their dad a hard time now and again, I have to admit. I bite my tongue, but all in all, they're pretty great. I love them, and that was kind of a surprise too. No, it's not the people involved." She let out a breath on a whoosh. "It's this. The house. His house. Their house. My house. Changing things. Decisions that can hurt kids' feelings without meaning to. I know it's been over six years since Holly passed away, but I'm sure they still miss her. I don't want to say or do anything that would mess with their healing."

"That's inevitable." Janet always spoke frankly, and today was no different. "I'd love to give you words of wisdom, but hurt feelings and raw emotions are unavoidable speed bumps in life."

Debbie knew the truth in that. She'd been engaged to a wonderful young man over two decades before. He'd been killed while serving overseas, and the heartbreak of what she'd lost had spurred her to stay in Cleveland when school ended. She didn't want to come back to Dennison and face constant reminders of dreams that could never become reality. Cleveland seemed easy by comparison, so she'd found an apartment and worked her way up the corporate ladder.

Her stay there began because of her loss. Then it became more like corporate entrenchment. Season by season, goal after goal, year after year, until she finally hit the pause button and realized that life—real life, filled with family and friends—was passing her by. She folded her corporate tent, co-invested in a café tucked in the western end of the old Dennison train depot, and here she was. Engaged, soon to be married, and surveying a tangled mess of old growth and new sprouts.

"I'm happy to help you with this." Janet slipped her arm through Debbie's. "It looks like a stretch of nice weather starting on Saturday. How about we dive into this then? If we focus on one section at a time, I think we can have things shaped up by the beginning of May."

That was a month away. A busy month away. "That long? Really?"

"Sooner, if we work in the evenings too. But it's still chilly once the sun starts to head toward the horizon. Plus your schedule is cranking up."

Janet was right. She was just realizing that a spring sports calendar filled quickly when teenagers played on school teams. She and Greg were in the middle of planning a wedding. A big wedding on a short timeline. She wasn't after the perfect affair...

But she was hoping for *kind* of perfect because it *was* her wedding. And a wedding should always be a big deal.

The boys' baseball schedules had stacked up after a series of canceled games due to the rainy weather. Going to their games, cheering them on, took precedence.

Business was good and growing at a rate they'd never expected for year two at the Whistle Stop Café. She wasn't a shrinking violet, and she never shirked a good day's work, but tackling the mess of gardens on top of everything else this month might be foolish. She said as much to Janet, and Janet arched a brow. "Why foolish?"

"It feels like a silly thing to worry about now, with so much else to do. So many decisions to make. I had no idea that planning a wedding involved this many options and meetings. It's not like you just pick this and choose that. It's all about comparison shopping, price points, and even escape clauses."

"You're planning an escape?"

Debbie saw Janet's look of amusement, and rolled her eyes. "Not on a personal level, but if there's a natural disaster or some dreadful illness or something, a good contract has an escape clause. A bow-out clause."

Janet opened her mouth to reply, but Cecily Markham Haygood's car pulled into the driveway right then. An avid member of the local historical society and garden club, Cecily lived north of Greg's house in a picture-perfect classic colonial. Her two-story home was set back far enough to have a gracious front yard but not so far that her lush gardens weren't ogled and admired by passersby. The strategically curved plantings were symmetrically balanced with a perfect sun-to-shade ratio on the three visible sides of her lovely home. Debbie knew this because Cecily had explained it. More than once.

Cecily loved Dennison, history, and horticulture. For seven months of the year she worked at the big garden center in New Philadelphia. When it came to pretty yards, Cecily stepped out with tornadic knowledge about everything to do with landscaping on any scale. It was information she avidly shared with anyone who would listen. The last thing Debbie wanted right now was a lecture.

She had eyes. She saw what a wreck the gardens were, but—

She cringed inside as Cecily crossed the driveway with her recognizable firm step. When Cecily paused alongside Debbie, the older woman drew her brows together and pressed her mouth into a tight, thin line. She took a deep breath—and said nothing.

Debbie looked at Janet then back at Cecily.

Then she greeted her neighbor because that was about the only option left. "Cecily, hello. Nice of you to drop by during such a busy season at the garden center. You're just getting into the crazy time of year up there, aren't you?"

Cecily arched one brow. She did it so well that Debbie was sure she must practice the maneuver in front of a mirror. Then she handed Debbie a flyer. "Our biweekly sales at the center. I know Greg hasn't had time to tend to things the way he'd like to, but I also know that's likely to change now that there's going to be a woman in the house."

Debbie accepted the flyer but not the challenge. "This particular woman spent twenty years in a big city apartment, so I don't pretend to have knowledge of gardens, flowers, bushes, or pretty much anything outside aside from trees. I'm good with trees." She aimed a smile at Cecily. "But that's my extent."

Cecily was far too ladylike to show her displeasure. She leaned forward as if sharing a confidence. "And that's why we embrace every opportunity to learn that comes our way. I find women are better at that than men, but I don't say that to too many people, of course. I want you to know I'm available to give advice as needed, even though I'm pretty busy right now with my work and my family. Not to mention my civic duty. I've drawn up a petition to encourage our town leaders to clamp down on people parking monster-sized vehicles in their driveways all year. It's ridiculous and a hazard." She huffed, then changed the subject by directing her gaze to the borders flanking the Connor house. "Anyway, I look for potential. And Debbie Albright-soon-to-be-Connor, there is a wealth of potential surrounding you here. And—"

She stopped talking as Greg's younger son headed their way from the backyard. He carried the family's two garden gnomes, a boy and a girl. Greg had told her that the boys' mother had purchased the gnomes about ten years before. She'd dubbed them Hans and Greta, and the beloved pair claimed a spot in the front garden every year. Julian raised his right hand, the one holding "Greta," and spoke to Debbie. "Dad says supper's about ready and we can put the gnomes out now. He said the weather is mild enough so they'll be okay."

"Oh, they're adorable." Janet smiled at him. "They're like a little Dutch pair, Julian. Prettier than a lot of gnomes we see around."

"The words *pretty* and *gnome* should never be uttered together." Cecily sighed. "Although I see more and more of this kind of thing in the village and around the town. Gnomes, little signs, metal whatnots, and wooden flowers. As if God hasn't given us enough natural beauty, we feel the need to augment His green earth with a hodgepodge of manmade this-es and thats. I've a good mind to add banning lawn ornaments to my petition. It's like a springtime invasion that's growing worse every year."

Julian grinned at her. "But an awesome invasion, right? These were my mom's." He'd grown this past year. He was taller than Janet and Debbie and had Cecily by a good three inches. "She loved these guys."

"Understandably so." Debbie smiled at her soon-to-be stepson. "Tuck them in where you'd like them to be, and we'll shift them around as we clean things up. Okay?"

"Okay." He crossed the yard to place the two small statues on either side of the front garden plot. "Then I have homework from Miss McGinnity." The drama in his voice matched the expression on his thirteen-year-old face. "Book analysis. Why can't she just call it a book report like every other teacher in the world?" He frowned as he stood up once the statues were in place.

Janet winked at Debbie as Julian trudged back to the house. She had a college-age daughter and understood teen drama quite well. "I'm heading home to spread mulch. We'll figure this out." She reached out and gave Debbie a half hug. "Promise."

"And my offer of help is long-standing," Cecily said to Debbie. "It's different for artists, you know."

Debbie frowned because she had no idea what her neighbor meant.

Never at a loss for words, Cecily was quick to explain. "Artists can paint over a canvas to complete a new work. That option doesn't exist with gardens. Sometimes what they need is a full extraction. Then we begin again. Kind of a metaphor on life, isn't it?" She flashed Debbie a quick smile, then crossed the driveway to her car.

She'd blocked Janet in, so she backed out first.

Janet followed. Debbie stayed behind, mulling over the weeds, the lack of time, and a to-do list that rivaled any she'd ever dealt with before.

Julian came out the front door. He clutched a notebook and a paperback in his hands and had two pens stuffed in the side pocket of his hoodie. The pens tumbled out as he took a seat. They rolled, one after the other, hitting all three steps on their way to the side-walk below. He let out a woebegone sigh—quite overdone—as he stood to retrieve the pens. Then he sat back down, pulled a sheet of paper from the folder, and set it on his lap. "Addled with April."

He frowned, then folded his arms in a move so much like his father's that Debbie felt it inside. "How is anyone supposed to know what this means? Or care? What is Miss McGinnity thinking? 'He was addled with April. He was dizzy with spring. He was—'"

"'As drunk as Lem Forrester on a Saturday night.'" She finished the quote for him. When his brows shot up in surprise, she was pretty sure she'd scored a point with her fiancé's younger son. "Marjorie Kinnan Rawlings. *The Yearling*. Junior high required reading even when I was in school. Mrs. Anderson's Language Arts class."

He made no attempt to hide his astonishment. "How'd you remember that? It's so random."

"A more apt question is, how could I forget it?" She posed the question to him as she settled a kneeling pad onto the damp ground. The cushion made weeding easier on her clothes and her knees. "One of the best-written coming-of-age books. Right up there with *Where the Red Fern Grows*."

Julian had solid reading skills. "I liked a lot of books when I was a kid," he told Debbie frankly.

She fought a smile because clearly thirteen was well beyond "kid" stage in Julian's mindset.

"Funny ones, fantasy ones, all kinds of stuff. The Fisher twins were my favorites for a long time, but now I'd rather read books about real life people who do great things," he continued. "Jackie Robinson. Harriet Tubman. Abe Lincoln. Anyway, I don't know why it has to rain nonstop. So many games have been rained out, and we end up having to play a bunch of them all at once. That makes the pitching schedule crazy because you're only allowed so many innings in middle school. I just wanna play baseball."

Today's games had been canceled due to wet field conditions, and Greg had asked Julian to give her a hand in the front garden. A break in the rain had offered them a brief window. The rain had softened the soil, making weeding a bit easier, and she and Julian had tackled those when he got home from school.

Debbie wasn't just a non-gardener with zero experience. She'd spent twenty years in a Cleveland high rise and killed every house-plant she'd ever received. If she was given one by an unknowing person the final five years of her stay there, she quickly regifted the plant to someone else as a gesture of mercy.

Julian rested his elbow on one knee and propped his chin on his hand, glum.

"I've always liked a book that makes me run the full gamut of emotions," she told him. She knelt on the pad, ready to start near the sidewalk. "Laugh, cry, mourn. But I expect that rubs salt in the wound when you've lost someone so close to you."

Julian straightened. "You lost someone you loved."

She lifted her gaze to his.

"The guy you were going to marry when you were in college. But you *still* like those books. I don't get it."

"I read them before I'd lost anyone close to me," she replied. "Big difference."

"I guess." He sighed again. "Mrs. Haywood's granddaughter is coming over to do this assignment with me. Kelsey."

"Kelsey Addison. Her dad owns the mechanic shop on the far side of town."

"And her other grandparents own the big farm with all the donkeys."

Debbie knew Claymont Farm well. She and Janet had gone to school with Dani Addison, and they'd recently helped her figure out who was sabotaging their family farm. That hadn't been an easy thing to puzzle out, but they'd persevered. "I love that farm."

"It's cool. They make really good doughnuts."

There was an understandable adolescent perspective.

"Anyway, I don't know why they have to assign homework on weeknights. Or even at all. Or why we have to have partners. I don't need a partner. Partners have too many ideas. But Kelsey knows how to do stuff with a computer that makes the reports look cool."

"Due tomorrow?" she asked.

"Monday."

"That gives you plenty of time," Greg said as he came out the front door. He had a bag slung over his left arm. "There's a problem at the church. A plumbing mishap. It shouldn't take long. Julian, do you want to come along and help?"

Julian shook his head. "I've got to get this done."

Debbie stayed quiet.

It was Tuesday. He had nearly a week to complete an assignment that could probably be done in an hour, but Greg didn't like to force the boys to join him with his jobs. If they volunteered, that was great, but he wanted their assistance to be on their terms. She understood his point, although she wished the boys would help their father more.

Jaxon came around the side of the house, shrugging into a light-weight hoodie. "I'll come, Dad."

Greg sent him a grateful look. "Sweet. I could use an extra pair of hands. Pastor Nick has a Bible study tonight, otherwise he'd help me set this straight." He turned back to Debbie. "You and Julian can go ahead and eat without us. We'll warm it up when we get home."

Julian didn't move until his father and brother had pulled out of the driveway. Then he stood and dusted off the seat of his pants. "I'm going inside. You wanna eat now?"

"Nah. I'm not all that hungry yet. I'll come in soon. You said Kelsey was coming over?"

He nodded. "In like an hour."

Debbie waited.

He didn't really want to help her, and he didn't want to help his father.

He wanted to play baseball. Three straight days of rain had thwarted his game and practice schedule that week. But Debbie wasn't in charge of the weather, and life offered its share of disappointments. "If you want to help me attack this section, we could call it quits in twenty minutes and have supper together."

He glanced at the gardens bordering the front steps. "I don't think they look too bad. Not really."

"That's code for 'I don't want to get on my hands and knees on the cold, wet ground and pull weeds,' right?"

He fought a smile. "Pretty much."

"Go on in. I got this," she told him. "I'm always ready for spring in February. The fact that winter hangs around until the end of March is a five-week annoyance, but at least spring comes earlier here. Earlier than near the lake in Cleveland, anyway." She pretended to shiver. "Winter holds on there until May, and you know what that does?"

Julian shook his head.

"It makes people grumpy. No one wants to be freezing in April and May. At least we get a couple of softer weeks in southern Ohio. Can you go across the front there and straighten Greta? She's tipping."

"Sure." He took the route across the grass. He lifted the gnome, then carefully flattened the ground below before snugging her into place in front of a rosebush. The rosebush was another thing Debbie recognized. She gave herself extra points for that.

"Mom wasn't a fan of loading up gardens with goofy things, but she liked these two little gnomes."

"Because they're cute. Like you."

Julian ignored that remark, gave the gnomes one last look, then headed for the house.

Amelia Addison swung by with Kelsey as scheduled. The eighth grader hopped out of the car and started for the house, but paused when Amelia rolled down the passenger window. "Eight o'clock, right? Hey, Debbie, how are you?"

Debbie had stood when the car pulled in. Her knees protested the move in spite of the pad she'd set on the ground. She was pretty sure she'd used muscles she hadn't used in a long time, because a fair share of them hurt.

She smiled at Amelia as she rubbed a hand to the small of her back. "I'll be better with a mild painkiller and some muscle rub. Hands-and-knees gardening isn't for wimps."

Amelia laughed. "True. I've got plenty to do myself once I find a window of time. So, Kelsey. Eight?" She redirected her attention to her daughter.

Kelsey had politely waited until their conversation paused before answering her mother. "Eight's good. I'm going to show Julian how easy it is to create a report that Miss McGinnity will love so much that she can't help but give it an A." She patted the small bag she had slung over her shoulder and hurried for the side door.

"She's got a techie brain, that one." Amelia smiled as she watched Kelsey disappear through the door. "Like her dad. Always wondering how to fix this or adjust that or how things work. I like building things."

Amelia had a fine carpentry business that was doing well.

"Do you want me to drop her off at your house?" offered Debbie. "I'll be heading back to my place about then."

"I'm going to be right up the road at Mom and Dad's place, but thank you. I appreciate the offer. Mom's doing up a petition to urge the town to reconsider what people can put in their driveways. It's been a constant discussion since the weather started to break. She's on a mission, and when my mother is on a mission, no one and nothing stands in the way." Amelia grinned. "Good thing she's got a big heart or she'd be unbearable, but she does so much good for everyone she meets that they mostly overlook her bossiness. See you later."

"Yes. And good luck," Debbie teased.

Amelia laughed and backed out of the driveway.

The effect of a cute girl on Julian's homework attitude was a noticeable change for the better. Greg and Jaxon pulled in as Debbie was preparing to go home. Hammer jumped out first. The black-and-white border collie loved riding shotgun. He bounded up the steps, paused for a petting, then followed Jaxon and the pizza he was carrying through the back door.

Greg gave her a rueful look. "It took longer than expected. I'm sorry. I wanted to spend more of the evening with you."

"Me too." She stretched up to kiss him. "But then there's tomorrow evening. And the next. And the—"

He laughed, caught her up, and spun her around. "And almost every evening after that."

"Yes." She laughed and moved to her car. "Julian and Kelsey finished the dreaded English assignment, and from the sounds of it they put together a really solid report. They have moved on to the Industrial Revolution. I believe they've arrived at an Edison vs. Tesla point in time. They seem to like the drama." She reached up and kissed him one more time. "Come see me at work tomorrow. I'll make you a delicious coffee. Or sandwich. Whatever you'd like." She started to climb into the seat, then paused.

The dusk-to-dawn lights were all on. The gardens still looked unkempt, so that wasn't what drew her attention.

Still...something...

Something looked wrong. Different. Like there was something missing. Then it hit her. "The gnome."

Greg had followed her to the car to shut the door for her. He frowned and turned. "What about it?"

"She's gone, Greg. Greta is gone."

He narrowed his gaze. "Probably fell over. I'll check it out." He started crossing the yard, but Debbie was already back out of the car. She caught up to him on the grass.

"She was tipping slightly," she explained. "Before we went in. Julian fixed her and put her right up against that rosebush, and now she's not there."

He frowned as he stared at the now-empty spot. "You're sure that's where she was?"

"Absolutely. She was there when I went inside just over an hour ago. Now she's gone." She didn't want to overreact. The little figure was a low-money item but heavy on the emotions. "Where did she go? Who would take her? She's a garden gnome. How did this happen?"

He looked as confused as she felt. "First we need to ask Julian if he moved her. If he didn't, it'll be easier to track her down in the morning. You're sure he put her here? By this bush?"

"Positive."

Greg sighed. "An April Fool's joke, maybe? A bad one?"

"An April Fool's joke that's not one bit funny." Debbie bit her lip, and Greg put his arm around her shoulders.

"She'll turn up. She couldn't have gotten too far, right? She *is* mobility challenged." He winked, but Debbie didn't miss the concern in his eyes. The pair of gnomes linked the past with the present. Something of Holly's. A funny, quirky thing the boys remembered. As the years went by, those memories were becoming scarcer, particularly for Julian because he'd been so young when she passed away.

"She could have gotten pretty far if someone stole her."

"Who steals gnomes?" Greg sounded doubtful. "There's a plethora of them all over these days. Old ones, fat ones, bearded ones. They're everywhere. I'll check with Ian to see if there's some new social media gnome challenge going on. That's the only thing that could explain something so random and crazy."

For some reason, the missing statue hit Debbie hard. Maybe because she'd been the last one in the yard? "Crazy or not, she's missing, and those gnomes are important to the boys."

"She'll turn up." He didn't want her to worry, but she wasn't born yesterday. The gnome had been there just an hour ago. Now it was gone. And since gnomes couldn't walk, someone had taken little Greta from her niche in the garden. Debbie was determined to find out who had that kind of nerve. Even on April Fool's Day.

A NOTE FROM the EDITORS

We hope you enjoyed another exciting volume in the Whistle Stop Café Mysteries series, published by Guideposts. For over seventy-five years, Guideposts, a nonprofit organization, has been driven by a vision of a world filled with hope. We aspire to be the voice of a trusted friend, a friend who makes you feel more hopeful and connected.

By making a purchase from Guideposts, you join our community in touching millions of lives, inspiring them to believe that all things are possible through faith, hope, and prayer. Your continued support allows us to provide uplifting resources to those in need. Whether through our communities, websites, apps, or publications, we inspire our audiences, bring them together, and comfort, uplift, entertain, and guide them. Visit us at guideposts.org to learn more.

We would love to hear from you. Write us at Guideposts, P.O. Box 5815, Harlan, Iowa 51593 or call us at (800) 932-2145. Did you love *Sooner or Later*? Leave a review for this product on guideposts. org/shop. Your feedback helps others in our community find relevant products.

Find inspiration, find faith, find Guideposts.

Shop our best sellers and favorites at
guideposts.org/shop

Or scan the QR code to go directly to our Shop

**While you are waiting for the next fascinating story
in the Whistle Stop Café Mysteries, check out
some other Guideposts mystery series!**

SECRETS FROM
GRANDMA'S ATTIC

Life is recorded not only in decades or years, but in events and memories that form the fabric of our being. Follow Tracy Doyle, Amy Allen, and Robin Davisson, the granddaughters of the recently deceased centenarian, Pearl Allen, as they explore the treasures found in the attic of Grandma Pearl's Victorian home, nestled near the banks of the Mississippi in Canton, Missouri. Not only do Pearl's descendants uncover a long-buried mystery at every attic exploration, they also discover their grandmother's legacy of deep, abiding faith, which has shaped and guided their family through the years. These uncovered Secrets from Grandma's Attic reveal stories of faith, redemption, and second chances that capture your heart long after you turn the last page.

History Lost and Found
The Art of Deception
Testament to a Patriot
Buttoned Up

Pearl of Great Price

Hidden Riches

Movers and Shakers

The Eye of the Cat

Refined by Fire

The Prince and the Popper

Something Shady

Duel Threat

A Royal Tea

The Heart of a Hero

Fractured Beauty

A Shadowy Past

In Its Time

Nothing Gold Can Stay

The Cameo Clue

Veiled Intentions

Turn Back the Dial

A Marathon of Kindness

A Thief in the Night

Coming Home

SAVANNAH SECRETS

Welcome to Savannah, Georgia, a picture-perfect Southern city known for its manicured parks, moss-covered oaks, and antebellum architecture. Walk down one of the cobblestone streets, and you'll come upon Magnolia Investigations. It is here where two friends have joined forces to unravel some of Savannah's deepest secrets. Tag along as clues are exposed, red herrings discarded, and thrilling surprises revealed. Find inspiration in the special bond between Meredith Bellefontaine and Julia Foley. Cheer the friends on as they listen to their hearts and rely on their faith to solve each new case that comes their way.

The Hidden Gate
A Fallen Petal
Double Trouble
Whispering Bells
Where Time Stood Still
The Weight of Years
Willful Transgressions
Season's Meetings
Southern Fried Secrets
The Greatest of These
Patterns of Deception

The Waving Girl
Beneath a Dragon Moon
Garden Variety Crimes
Meant for Good
A Bone to Pick
Honeybees & Legacies
True Grits
Sapphire Secret
Jingle Bell Heist
Buried Secrets
A Puzzle of Pearls
Facing the Facts
Resurrecting Trouble
Forever and a Day

MYSTERIES of MARTHA'S VINEYARD

Priscilla Latham Grant has inherited a lighthouse! So with not much more than a strong will and a sore heart, the recent widow says goodbye to her lifelong Kansas home and heads to the quaint and historic island of Martha's Vineyard, Massachusetts. There, she comes face-to-face with adventures, which include her trusty canine friend, Jake, three delightful cousins she didn't know she had, and Gerald O'Bannon, a handsome coast guard captain—plus head-scratching mysteries that crop up with surprising regularity.

A Light in the Darkness
Like a Fish Out of Water
Adrift
Maiden of the Mist
Making Waves
Don't Rock the Boat
A Port in the Storm
Thicker Than Water
Swept Away
Bridge Over Troubled Waters
Smoke on the Water
Shifting Sands
Shark Bait
Seascape in Shadows

Storm Tide
Water Flows Uphill
Catch of the Day
Beyond the Sea
Wider Than an Ocean
Sheeps Passing in the Night
Sail Away Home
Waves of Doubt
Lifeline
Flotsam & Jetsam
Just Over the Horizon

Find more inspiring stories in these best-loved Guideposts fiction series!

Mysteries of Lancaster County

Follow the Classen sisters as they unravel clues and uncover hidden secrets in Mysteries of Lancaster County. As you get to know these women and their friends, you'll see how God brings each of them together for a fresh start in life.

Secrets of Wayfarers Inn

Retired schoolteachers find themselves owners of an old warehouse-turned-inn that is filled with hidden passages, buried secrets, and stunning surprises that will set them on a course to puzzling mysteries from the Underground Railroad.

Tearoom Mysteries Series

Mix one stately Victorian home, a charming lakeside town in Maine, and two adventurous cousins with a passion for tea and hospitality. Add a large scoop of intriguing mystery, and sprinkle generously with faith, family, and friends, and you have the recipe for *Tearoom Mysteries*.

Ordinary Women of the Bible

Richly imagined stories—based on facts from the Bible—have all the plot twists and suspense of a great mystery, while bringing you fascinating insights on what it was like to be a woman living in the ancient world.

To learn more about these books, visit Guideposts.org/Shop